CAN WE TALK ABOUT RACE?

CAN WE TALK ABOUT RACE?

And Other Conversations in an
Era of School Resegregation

BEVERLY DANIEL TATUM, PH.D.

A Simmons College / Beacon Press
Race, Education, and Democracy Series Book

Beacon Press
Boston

Beacon Press
25 Beacon Street
Boston, Massachusetts 02108-2892
www.beacon.org

Beacon Press books
are published under the auspices of
the Unitarian Universalist Association of Congregations.

This book is published as part of the Simmons College/Beacon Press
Race, Education, and Democracy Lecture and Book Series, and is based
on lectures delivered at Simmons College in 2006.

11 10   8 7 6 5 4

This book is printed on acid-free paper that meets the uncoated paper
ANSI/NISO specifications for permanence as revised in 1992.

Text design by Tag Savage at Wilsted & Taylor Publishing Services
Composition by Wilsted & Taylor Publishing Services

LOC number 2007922270
ISBN 978-0-8070-3285-5

To Constance, C. Delores, Rosa, Coretta, and the women of Spelman who will follow them

CONTENTS

Can We Talk about Race?

When I was invited in the summer of 2005 to start imagining this book as the first in the Race, Education, and Democracy series, I did not know in a conscious way that we were nearing the end of an era. I did not know that the next few months would be punctuated by the passing of a generation of Black women who had devoted their lives to the struggle for civil and human rights—women who had been empowered by their own education to work toward the elimination of racism and create a more inclusive vision of democracy—women like Constance Baker Motley, a distinguished civil rights lawyer who wrote the original complaint in the *Brown v. Board of Education* Supreme Court case; C. Delores Tucker, a tireless civil rights activist and founder of the National Congress of Black Women; Rosa Louise Parks, whose courageous refusal to give up her seat on an Alabama bus in 1955 changed the world; and Coretta Scott King, an icon of the civil rights movement who not only fought to preserve her husband's legacy but became a tireless advocate for justice and human rights in her own right.

Indeed, it was just a few days after the passing of Mrs. King on January 30, 2006, that I gave my first Race, Education, and

Democracy lecture at Simmons College, represented here as Chapter One, "The Resegregation of Our Schools and the Affirmation of Identity." I was privileged to attend Mrs. King's funeral in Atlanta, and as I sat in the church listening to the dignitaries who had assembled to honor her memory, I thought about all the ways in which our society has changed since she and Martin Luther King Jr. left Boston in 1954 to begin their married lives in Montgomery, Alabama, and the bus boycott launched by Rosa Parks's actions in 1955. Their deaths, and those of the other women, represent the passing away of a generation raised under the iron rule of legalized segregation, a generation whose time and place must seem, to many young people, far removed from our current reality. Yet despite their courageous leadership and sacrifice, and the courage and sacrifice of many others, more than fifty years later we find ourselves still confronting the legacy of race and racism in our society, particularly in our schools, a reality that undermines the quality of education for all students and represents an ongoing threat to the fabric of our democracy.

Perhaps this should not surprise us. Martin Luther King Jr. once said, "The arc of the moral universe is long, but it bends toward justice." My parents left the South in 1958 to escape segregation, but I, like many African Americans in the "reverse migration" of the late twentieth and early twenty-first centuries, have returned to the South of my birth, and now live in Atlanta, Georgia, where I serve as president of Spelman College, the oldest continuing historically Black college for women. When I think of my daily experience at the malls of Atlanta, and in the hotels downtown, and at cultural events, it is sometimes easy to forget that Black people did not always have such easy access to restaurants, libraries, restrooms, and water fountains. Young people may not know that familiar department stores were sites of local protest. Yet it was only some

four decades ago that the Civil Rights Act of 1964 opened segregated public accommodations to "Negroes," as we were then
called. It is clear to see the way the arc has bent in my lifetime.

Yet as we celebrate what is undeniable progress, there is a
reality lurking in the shadows about which most of us are not
talking, and that is the resegregation of our public schools. The
fact of school resegregation and its implications for important
aspects of our democratic society lie at the core of each of the
essays included in this book. In essence, meaningful opportunities for cross-racial contact are diminishing, especially in
schools. What effect is that having on students, both White and
of color, and their teachers? What are the implications for classroom performance and academic achievement? Interpersonal
relations? Our evolving democracy? What can *we* as educators
and citizens do to ensure that the arc of the moral universe continues to bend toward justice in our society? These are the issues I have tried to address from my standpoint as an African
American female psychologist and educator who has been urging her students and colleagues to talk about race since I began
teaching a course on the psychology of racism in 1980. Here I
ask the fundamental question again: *Can we talk about race?*

This question can be asked and answered in multiple ways.
First, *can* we talk about race? Are we *allowed* to do so? We are
living in a unique moment of legal history in which the notion
of considering race (talking about race) in school admissions is
being challenged at the K–12 level as well as in higher education. I chronicle the legal history that has brought us from the
Brown v. Board of Education decision of 1954 to *Grutter v. Bollinger* in 2003 (the case that upheld the use of racial consideration in admissions at the University of Michigan Law School)
and now to *Parents Involved in Community Schools v. Seattle
School District No. 1* and *Meredith v. Jefferson County Board of
Education et al.,* two cases involving the use of racial considera-

tion to maintain diversity in public schools, taken under consideration by the Supreme Court in December 2006. The Court's decision was still pending as this book went to press in early 2007. Even as the Supreme Court considered the limitations of the equal protection clause of the Fourteenth Amendment, we were watching voters in states like California and Michigan approve so-called civil rights initiatives designed to prohibit any such affirmative action programs.[1] *Can* we talk about race?

Ironically, as U.S. secretary of education Margaret Spellings advocates for the elimination of racial consideration in school admissions throughout our system of education, the No Child Left Behind (NCLB) Act, signed into law in 2002, requires that we talk about race. The NCLB legislation requires among other things that schools disaggregate the test scores of all students along racial lines. The purpose of doing so is to make sure that all children are succeeding in school—to ensure that the failures of some are not being camouflaged by the success of others, hidden in school averages that reduce accountability and recognition of achievement problems that need to be addressed. One result is that we talk frequently about racial differences in performance. Newspapers regularly report test disparities in school districts along racial and ethnic lines, reinforcing the public perception of inadequate school performance on the part of many Black and Hispanic students. However, we don't talk often enough about the way the return to school resegregation has confined so many students of color to high-poverty schools where high teacher turnover also means a steady influx of novice teachers, placing vulnerable children in the hands of those perhaps least prepared to give them what they need.[2] In the same way, our public discourse rarely turns to the way our conceptions of race, intelligence, testing, and expectations might impact those disparities. It is that conversation that I present in Chapter Two, "Connecting the Dots: How Race in America's Classrooms Affects Achievement."

Can we talk about race? Do we know how? Does the childhood segregation of our schools and neighborhoods and the silence about race in our culture inhibit our capacity to have meaningful dialogue with others, particularly in the context of cross-racial relationships? Can we get beyond our fear, our sweaty palms, our anxiety about saying the wrong thing, or using the wrong words, and have an honest conversation about racial issues? What does it mean in our personal and professional lives when we can't? This is the question that I explore in Chapter Three, "'What Kind of Friendship Is That?': The Search for Authenticity, Mutuality, and Social Transformation in Cross-Racial Relationships," as I consider the dynamics of cross-racial friendship in a society that does not encourage—indeed actively *discourages*—talk about race.

Can *we* talk about race? By "we" I mean those of us who are in leadership positions in education—as faculty, as administrators, as men and women of influence. Are we able to serve as role models to young people who may not have the benefit of the educational diversity we have experienced in our lives? Do they see us as able to cross racial and ethnic boundaries to connect with others different from ourselves?

The southern region I live in today is different in many ways from the one my parents left in 1958, and it was students who helped change it. Willie Mays, James Felder, Marlon Bennett, Don Clarke, Mary Ann Smith, and Roslyn Pope were the student government presidents of Atlanta University, Clark College, Interdenominational Theological Center (ITC), Morehouse College, Morris Brown College, and Spelman College, respectively. In 1960 these six students placed a full-page ad in the *Atlanta Constitution* titled "An Appeal for Human Rights."[3]

A powerful and courageous statement, it challenged segregation in federally funded hospitals, and in schools, highlighted the absence of Black police and firefighters, raised questions about inequities in school funding, and protested the fact that many were still being denied the right to vote. Their ad signaled the beginning of several years of highly visible student activism—sit-ins, kneel-ins, marches, and other forms of nonviolent protest. These young people were committed to bending the arc of the moral universe just a little faster. They used their education to challenge the status quo and build a better society. How will this generation of students use theirs?

Unlike K–12 education, colleges and universities are still "desegregating"—at least for now. How can we use this window of opportunity to inspire the next generation to take responsibility for creating a more *inclusive* rather than *exclusive* social order? Can we use this window of opportunity to mobilize the next generation of change agents? That is the task at hand, and the subject of Chapter Four, "In Search of Wisdom: Higher Education for a Changing Democracy."

A note about language: When we talk about race, who are we talking about? As I have discussed at length in an earlier book,[4] the concept of race itself is a faulty one. While we still make racial distinctions in our society, those distinctions are socially meaningful but not biologically valid. Biologists tell us that the only truly meaningful racial categorization is that of "human." Yet we still use the language of race, and need to, in order to describe what is taking place in the lives of particular groups of people, groups that have been socially defined on the basis of physical criteria, including skin color and facial features.[5] When we talk about school desegregation and resegregation, the conversation is often focused in terms of Black-White interaction, because *Brown v. Board of Education* addressed the exclusion of Black children from White schools, and that focus is also evident in this book. In discussing those experiences, I often use the terms "Black" and "African American" interchangeably.

However, the experience of exclusion from educational opportunity is not limited to Black children. Latinos share that history, particularly in Texas. The Hispanic population is growing rapidly throughout the country, but particularly in the South, where Latinos have very low rates of high school completion and college attendance.[6] Although Blacks and Latinos are often referred to as distinct groups, there is overlap in this population because Latinos have multiracial origins including combinations of European, African, and indigenous American Indian ancestry. Particularly when discussing urban school experiences, I often refer to Black and Latino children together because there are many similarities in their struggle for access to educational equity. While there is little discussion about the unique situation of either Native Americans or Asian Americans in this collection of essays, both groups have also had experiences with discrimination in schooling, particularly in the regions where those populations have been most concentrated.[7] When I use the terms "people of color" or "students of color," as I do throughout the book, it is my intention to include in that language all of the racial and ethnic minority groups I have mentioned here, and when I use the term "White" I am referring to people of European ancestry who have historically benefited from the privileges associated with light skin in our still-color-conscious society. I am aware as I write this introduction that the issues I have written about in the chapters to follow are complex and that there is more to say than I have been able to include in these pages. It is my hope that the reader will find these essays a source of stimulation for further reading and dialogue with others. We need a conversation, and time is running out. I say that time is running out because we as a nation have a lot of problems to solve, and we need an educated citizenry if we are to address those problems.

Thomas Friedman, author of *The World Is Flat,* describes the global advances in education and technology that threaten the American economy, yet he offers the hope of innovation as a wellspring for American competitiveness.[8] In this information age, in order to innovate you need intellectually curious people who have been well educated, particularly in the areas of science and technology. While many are looking beyond our borders for that talent as the White birth rate declines, it is the rising generation of students of color and those that follow them that will be our national supply of talent. We have to talk about the way that our socialization about race prevents us from fully recognizing that talent, and the way that the dynamics of race in our society have kept us from fully educating youth of color. If we don't fully engage in dialogue about what we can do differently, and bring an understanding of the legacy of race and racism in our society into that conversation, we will not be successful in addressing this and other national challenges. We have a wealth of untapped and underutilized talent in communities of color across the country; we need this talent. *Can we talk about race?*

ONE

The Resegregation of Our Schools and the Affirmation of Identity

In September 2004, I celebrated my fiftieth birthday—a significant occasion under any circumstance, but it felt especially so because it coincided with the observation of the fiftieth anniversary of *Brown v. Board of Education*. It gave me the opportunity to reflect not only on what I optimistically regard as the first half of my life, but also on the significance of having been born in 1954, just a few months after that momentous Supreme Court decision outlawing the "separate but equal" doctrine of segregation. I often call myself an "integration baby," because the struggle to desegregate American educational institutions has shaped my life from the beginning. I entered the world in Tallahassee, Florida, where my father, Robert Daniel, taught in the art department at Florida A&M University. Eager to obtain a doctorate in art education, my father hoped to study at nearby Florida State University, but in 1954 the State of Florida still refused to open the doors of FSU to an African American graduate student. Instead the state paid his travel expenses to Pennsylvania rather than desegregate the Florida graduate program. In 1957 he completed his degree at Penn State. A year later he became the first African American professor at Bridgewater State College in Bridgewater, Massachusetts, the community where I grew up. There the ideal of integration was more often the reality of tokenism, as I was frequently the only Black student in my class.

For those who were in school in the 1950s, it is not hard to recall the inequities associated with school segregation. However, when I think of my own children, both born in the 1980s, I realize that the civil rights struggle of the 1950s and 1960s is seen as a set of events in a far distant past. It is worth reminding them that it was not so long ago. As I have said to my children, it was all in my lifetime, and I am not that old.

Certainly we know that the "separate but equal" doctrine —which legally sanctioned segregated schools while spuriously promising equal educational opportunity—ensured separation but never provided equality of resources. Southern states routinely spent more money on White schools than on those serving Black children. According to data presented by Charles Clotfelter in his 2004 book, *After Brown: The Rise and Retreat of School Desegregation,* the differences were apparent in the quality of the facilities, the training of the teachers, the equipment available, the size of the classes, and the courses offered. For example, in 1945 the state of Mississippi had 2,120 one-room, one-teacher schools, and while only 50 percent of the students in the state were Black, 95 percent of the one-room schools were attended by Black students. While 54 percent of the teachers in the White schools in Mississippi were college graduates, only 10 percent of those in the Black schools were. Or consider the example of Durham, North Carolina, in 1950, where the White schools had gymnasiums and music and art rooms, while not one Black school had such facilities. The science laboratory in the White high school had 136 pieces of lab equipment, while the Black school science laboratory had only 21.[1]

Although these are southern examples, legalized segregation was not limited to the South. In addition to Alabama, Arkansas, Florida, Georgia, Louisiana, Mississippi, North and South Carolina, Tennessee, Texas, and Virginia (the eleven former Confederate states), the border states (Delaware, Kentucky, Maryland, Missouri, Oklahoma, West Virginia) and the District of Columbia also required school segregation. Prior to the 1950s, even in the West and the North there were states that had school districts requiring school segregation. Arizona, New Mexico, Kansas, Wyoming, Indiana, New Jersey, New York, and Pennsylvania all were in that category.[2]

In those states where there were no laws requiring segregation, separation still occurred because of residential housing patterns. Such patterns were not accidental, the result of free-market selection on the part of homebuyers. On the contrary, these patterns were the orchestrated result of housing ordinances, and the racial steering of real estate brokers, the lending practices of bankers, and the collective actions of White homeowners. Clotfelter writes,

> One of the most potent tools for maintaining residential segregation, a California innovation of the 1890s that was approved by the Supreme Court in 1926 and used widely following World War II, was the restrictive covenant, the insertion into deeds the promise not to sell a property to Blacks or members of other specified groups. Although ultimately declared unenforceable in 1948, its effects were solidified in the segregated patterns of residential development in the large cities of the North. More extreme was the practice of some suburban communities to exclude Blacks altogether.... Combined with other policies, in particular the selective location of public housing projects and the largely unchecked discrimination in the housing market, many of the urban areas of the

3

North became highly segregated. Perhaps the epitome of such segregation was Detroit, which as late as 1970 had fourteen suburban communities with populations of 36,000 or more, none of which had more than fifty Blacks. Such residential patterns led quite naturally to substantially segregated schools.[3]

In parts of California and Texas, Mexican American students were also subjected to systematic segregation, while the educational experience of Native Americans in the twentieth century was certainly shaped by the aftermath of the nineteenth-century creation of reservations and nonreservation boarding schools, designed to separate Indian children from family and tribal influences.[4] All were affected by the civil rights movement and the legacy of *Brown v. Board of Education*.

Although the *Brown* decision occurred in 1954, in 1955 the Supreme Court weakened its own decision by instructing the lower federal courts to "enter such orders and decrees consistent with this opinion as are necessary and proper to admit to public schools on a racially nondiscriminatory basis *with all deliberate speed* the parties to these cases."[5] The Harvard Law School professor Charles Ogletree, in his 2004 book, *All Deliberate Speed,* writes, "these three critical words would indeed turn out to be of great consequence, in that they ignore the urgency on which the Brown lawyers insisted. When asked to explain his view of 'all deliberate speed,' Thurgood Marshall frequently told anyone who would listen that the term meant S-L-O-W."[6]

In the 1950s and 1960s there was no reason to ask the question that in the 1990s became the title of my book: "Why are all the Black kids sitting together in the cafeteria?" The answer was self-evident. African Americans weren't *allowed* in the school, never mind the cafeteria, or, as in the case of Bridgewater, the small Massachusetts town where I grew up, there were so few Black students present in White schools, there weren't enough to fill a cafeteria table.

The pattern of widespread school segregation did not begin to change substantially until the passage of the Civil Rights Act of 1964. Not only did this congressional act open public accommodations such as restaurants, hotels, water fountains, and other public facilities to Black people, it also authorized the U.S. attorney general to bring lawsuits against school districts that were resisting the law, and allowed the secretary of Health, Education, and Welfare to withhold federal funds from any school district that was excluding students on the basis of race. On May 27, 1968, the Supreme Court finally put an end to the delay tactics of many southern school districts in *Green v. New Kent County.*[7] The historian Peter Irons writes:

> Justice William Brennan wrote for a unanimous Court that school districts were "clearly charged with the affirmative duty to take whatever steps may be necessary to convert to a unitary system in which racial discrimination would be eliminated root and branch."... A school district must "establish that its proposed plan promises meaningful and immediate progress toward disestablishing state-imposed segregation," and judges "should retain jurisdiction until it is clear that state-imposed segregation has been completely removed." Brennan drove the final nail into the coffin of "deliberate speed" as a delaying tactic. "The burden on a school board today," he wrote, "is to come forward with a plan that promises realistically to work, and promises realistically to work *now.*"[8]

And plans went into effect. Remarkable change occurred in the South in just a few years as the result of the desegregation plans implemented during the period between 1969 and 1972.

5

For example, in 1968, 78 percent of Black students in the South were enrolled in schools with 90 percent or more students of color. By 1972, only 25 percent of Black students in the South attended such highly segregated schools. In the early 1970s, urban school districts in the border states were also under court order to desegregate, with Oklahoma City and Prince George's County, Maryland, among the first to be affected by judicial action.[9] Busing orders were not limited to the South or the border states, however. Growing up in Massachusetts, I vividly remember watching the local news coverage of White Bostonians attacking school buses filled with Black children in response to court-ordered desegregation plans.

Change was also taking place in higher education—the 1970s marked the beginning of what we might call the "affirmative action" era in higher education, with many White institutions that had previously limited the enrollment of students of color now actively seeking to diversify their student bodies. I was one of those students they sought to recruit. I graduated from high school in 1971, an honors student with high SAT scores. Because I had grown up in a family of educators, college attendance was a clear expectation. Howard University, Morris College, Spelman College, Atlanta University (now known as Clark Atlanta), and Tuskegee University are all part of my family history—historically Black institutions where my parents, grandparents, and great-grandparents were educated. Had I graduated from high school ten years earlier, I probably would have followed in the family tradition of attending a historically Black college. However, in 1971 my mailbox was full of college offers from many predominantly White colleges, and given that the door of opportunity was now open, it seemed important to walk through.

What I have called here the "affirmative action era" officially began in 1965. The term "affirmative action" became part

6

of our language and legal system in 1965, when President Lyndon Johnson signed Executive Order 11246. This order required federal contractors to "take affirmative action to ensure that applicants are employed, and that employees are treated during employment without regard to their race, color, religion, sex, or national origin." By law, contractors were obligated to make a "good faith effort" to use procedures that would result in equal employment opportunity for historically disadvantaged groups. The groups targeted for this "affirmative action" were White women, and men and women of color (specifically defined by the federal government as American Indian/Alaska Natives, Asian or Pacific Islanders, Blacks, and Hispanics). In the 1970s, legislation broadened the protected groups to include persons with disabilities and Vietnam veterans. Although Executive Order 11246 required affirmative action, it did not specify exactly what affirmative action programs should look like.[10]

Given this lack of specificity, it is not surprising that there is great variety in the way affirmative action programs have been developed and implemented around the country.[11] The executive order had as its goal equal employment opportunity. But in practice, because of continuing patterns of discrimination, that goal could not be reached without positive steps—affirmative action—to create that equality of opportunity.[12] And in the 1970s, historically White institutions of higher education were taking positive steps—affirmative action—to extend opportunity to those who had been previously denied.

When I entered Wesleyan University in Middletown, Connecticut, as a first-year student in 1971, I was part of a cohort group of Black and Latino students who were infusing racial and ethnic diversity into the institution for the first time in any significant way. And most of us sat together in the cafeteria. Given the social history that I have reviewed, it is not surprising that we did. Both casual interracial contact and close inter-racial friendship are positively associated with having attended racially mixed schools as a child.[13] Most of us—born in the 1950s and coming of age in the 1960s and early 1970s—were children of Brown's promise, not its eventual implementation, and were products of segregated schools, as were our White classmates. My own experience of growing up as a young Black woman in a White community was not a common one then, and it had been socially isolating for me, especially in my adolescence. I was thrilled to escape it in college, and relished every day that I sat at the "Black table" in the cafeteria.

Why were we sitting together then? It was an affirmation —a time to relax—a creation of community based on a shared experience of being one of few in an environment unaccustomed to our presence. Did all Black students share in it? No. Were White students intentionally excluded from it? Not in any active way. They were not usually the focus of our attention. We were primarily interested in ourselves and the experience we were having as what W. E. B. DuBois would have called the "talented tenth," exploring our dual consciousness as young Black men and women in a predominantly White college setting.[14] We were having what has been described by the psychologist William Cross in the terms of racial identity development theory as an "immersion experience."[15] This particular phase of identity development is characterized by a strong desire to surround oneself with symbols of one's racial identity, and actively seek out opportunities to learn about one's own history and culture with the support of same-race peers. Anger and frustration experienced as the result of encounters with individual or institutional manifestations of racism might fuel the impulse to gather together, but the connections are sustained through the joyful exploration of one's own culture and

8

the positive affirmation of one's group. Such reasons are still relevant today, perhaps even more so in some places.

When I entered college in 1971, the opportunity for interracial contact was a new experience for most, but such opportunities were expanding in our public schools. Under President Johnson, the federal government began vigorously enforcing desegregation laws, and by 1970 the schools in the South were far more racially mixed than those in any other region of the United States. However, the election of President Richard Nixon in 1968 marked the end of such vigorous enforcement and the beginning of the ideological reconfiguration of the Supreme Court, with four Nixon appointees.[16]

In a tape-recorded conversation with the attorney general, John Mitchell, President Nixon discussed his criteria for selecting a new Supreme Court justice: "I'd say that our first requirement is have a southerner. The second requirement, he must be a conservative southerner.... I don't care if he's a Democrat or a Republican. Third, within the definition of conservative, he must be against busing, and against forced housing integration. Beyond that, he can do what he pleases."[17]

And indeed, in a 5–4 vote with the four Nixon appointees (Warren E. Burger, Harry A. Blackmun, Lewis F. Powell, and William H. Rehnquist) voting with the majority, the 1974 *Milliken v. Bradley* decision was the first of a series of Supreme Court decisions that moved away from the government's efforts to desegregate schools. In this case, the Court prohibited court-ordered busing across district lines unless there was proof that the actions of the school districts had created the racial disparities between them. In other words, the Black inner-city schools of Detroit could not be desegregated at the expense of suburban children, most of whom were White.[18] This ruling led to more busing *within* cities, creating a backlash among White working-class families who had not been able to afford the move to the suburbs. Nowhere was this more clearly visible than in Boston, Massachusetts, where the nightly news covered the racial violence associated with court-ordered efforts to desegregate the Boston public schools. "White flight" was the result. In 1970 the Boston public schools enrolled 96,000 students, 59,000 of whom were White. By 2000, only 9,300 White students remained in the Boston public schools, just 15 percent of the current total.[19]

Judicial oversight in Boston and other cities ended in 1990 on the heels of yet another pivotal Supreme Court decision, this one focused on Oklahoma.[20] The Oklahoma case began in 1961 as the result of a lawsuit to integrate the schools, which had been segregated by order of the state constitution ever since Oklahoma achieved statehood in 1907. In 1963 the federal judge Luther Bohanon ruled that the "dual" system of education be ended. The school board adopted a "neighborhood zoning" plan in response, but because of residential segregation (the end result of racially restrictive real-estate covenants supported by state and local law), the neighborhood zoning plan was ineffective. Finally, in 1972, because little progress toward desegregation had been made, Judge Bohanon ordered a busing plan designed to achieve racial balance. Five years later, in 1977, the Board of Education of Oklahoma City asked Judge Bohanon to close the case and he did, expressing his confidence that the board would continue to comply with constitutional desegregation requirements. However, in 1985 the school board reinstated the neighborhood zoning plan, and Robert Dowell and the other original plaintiffs asked that the case be reopened. In 1989 the Tenth Circuit Court of Appeals ruled in their favor, instructing the Oklahoma City school board to design a new plan to integrate the Oklahoma City schools. The school board appealed, and the case went before the Supreme Court. The

Court sent the case back to Judge Bohanon to decide whether the state had satisfied the original desegregation order. In the end, Judge Bohanon ruled in the state's favor and closed the case.[21]

In his book, *Jim Crow's Children,* Peter Irons concludes,

> With student assignments now based on the "neighborhood school" policy, Oklahoma City's schools have become even more racially separated. In the 2000 school year, Black students were the largest racial group, comprising 39 percent of public school enrollment, more than twice the city-wide Black population of 16 percent. White students made up 33 percent in 2000, while Hispanic students had become a growing minority at 20 percent. Substantially more than half of the city's Black children now attend majority-Black schools, with more than half of the White children in majority-White schools. The outcome of the *Dowell* case seemed to justify the gloomy prediction of Thurgood Marshall in his *Milliken* dissent, seventeen years earlier, that the Court's abandonment of the *Brown* decisions would result in America's urban areas being "divided up each into two cities—one White, the other Black," with the children in each divided city attending schools in which few of their classmates belong to a different race.[22]

Indeed, the *Board of Education of Oklahoma City v. Dowell* decision had the ripple effect of federal judges releasing other school districts from their court-ordered desegregation plans. This and other related court decisions in the 1990s have contributed to *increasing* rather than decreasing school segregation. This shift has been particularly striking in the South, in part because southern school districts made the most visible progress toward desegregation in the 1970s and 1980s, even in rural

11

areas that had seemed particularly resistant in the early days of the civil rights era. However, in the 1990s, the Supreme Court moved from a period of setting limits on desegregation methods (as in *Milliken*) to what Gary Orfield, the director of the Harvard Civil Rights Project, has called a "period of retreat and reversal," symbolized by decisions such as *Board of Education of Oklahoma City,* which supported resegregation. In response, for the first time since the 1954 *Brown v. Board of Education* decision, segregation in southern public schools is steadily increasing, and has been for more than a decade, while the largely intractable segregation of northern cities has intensified.[23]

BEYOND THE MYTH OF SCHOOL INTEGRATION

While this brief overview of fifty years of judicial decisions and educational impact may be quite familiar to some of my generation, I focus on it here because there are many people who may remember *Brown v. Board of Education* but who have no recollection of *Milliken v. Bradley* or *Board of Education of Oklahoma City v. Dowell* or the other Supreme Court decisions that collectively facilitated the return to public school segregation. As a culture, we celebrate the symbolic importance of the anniversary of *Brown v. Board of Education,* without fully acknowledging the reality of K–12 public school resegregation. We need to understand this recent history and its implications for schooling in our society today.

If our focus is on the multiracial representations of a few evening TV dramas, or the increasing presence of people of color in many work environments, or the discourse of diversity in the popular culture around us, we might easily labor under the assumption that we now live, work, and go to school in an integrated society. But for many in the United States, that simply is not true. According to the 2004 Census data, the U.S. population is now approximately 67.4 percent non-Hispanic White, 14 percent Hispanic, 12.8 percent Black, 4.2 percent Asian American, 1.2 percent American Indian, Alaska Native, or Pacific Islander; 1.5 percent of census participants identified themselves as belonging to "two or more races."[24] That diversity, however, is not reflected in most neighborhoods. Certainly as immigration increases in our border states and the population of color multiplies in cities across the nation, one can find a rich urban mosaic of varying cultures and ethnicities, but more often than not, these diverse cultural communities are separated neighborhood by neighborhood, and often school by school. Most African Americans, Latinos, and Whites still live in neighborhoods with people from their same racial group.[25]

Racial segregation is also associated with economic segregation. In 2000, 76 percent of those living in neighborhoods of concentrated poverty were Black or Latino. While Black-White residential segregation declined somewhat between 1980 and 2000, Blacks continue to experience the most residential segregation (as compared to other groups of color).[26] Approximately one-third of all Blacks live in neighborhoods of concentrated poverty.[27] Black-White residential segregation is highest in the Northeast and Midwest, a factor in the intensity of school segregation in those regions.

It is clear that those of us who came of age in the 1960s and 1970s are products of a historically unique period of progress toward integration that is not widely shared by young people today. As educators, it is important for us to understand the resegregating experience of students today and what it means for our educational practice and our society as a whole.

What is the significance of continuing residential segregation and increasing school resegregation? One possible outcome is that while interracial contact and more-tolerant racial attitudes increased during the last half of the twentieth century, the same may not be true in the first quarter of the twenty-first century, particularly in our public schools. For example, when high school students were asked, as part of an annual survey, how often they interacted with people of other races—engaging in activities such as having a conversation, eating together, or playing sports—the percentage of White students who said they did this "a lot" increased significantly over the time between 1976 and 2000, doubling from approximately 15 percent to 30 percent.[28] While conversely this statistic suggests that 70 percent of White youth do *not* have such experiences with great frequency, the increase in interaction reported in this study can be seen as a positive result of improving race relations in America. What will the answers be in 2010? In 2020?

For both Whites and Blacks, the likelihood of having either a multiracial social network of acquaintances or at least one close interracial friendship was linked to the experience of attending racially mixed schools in childhood.[29] As school districts move back to neighborhood school policies, the next generation of White students will likely have *less* school contact with people of color than their predecessors did. Particularly for young White children, interaction with people of color is likely to be a *virtual* reality rather than an *actual* one, with media images (often negative ones) most clearly shaping their attitudes and perceived knowledge of communities of color. The progress that has been made in the reduction of racial prejudice that can be associated with shared school experiences is at risk of stalling.

For students of color, the return to segregation means the increased likelihood of attending a school with limited resources. We know that 90 percent of highly segregated Black and Latino schools have high percentages of poor children; however, at most highly segregated White schools, middle-class students are in the majority.[30] The negative educational impact of attending high-poverty schools is well documented. Whether a student comes from a poor or middle-income family, academic achievement is likely to decline if the student attends a high-poverty school. Conversely, academic performance is likely to improve if the student attends a middle-class school, even if his or her own family is poor.[31]

The learning conditions that are taken for granted in middle-class suburban schools are too often absent in impoverished classrooms. As an example, the American Civil Liberties Union filed suit in 2000 against the State of California on behalf of children in eighteen public school districts, charging that children who attend schools without such basics as sufficient books, materials, working bathroom facilities, clean and safe buildings, trained teachers, and enough seats for every child are being denied their fundamental right to an education. In this case, 96.4 percent of the children affected by these dismal conditions were children of color, even though as a group, children of color represent only 59 percent of the public school population in California.[32] It is not surprising that the outcomes associated with high-poverty schools across the country are bleak: lower test scores, higher dropout rates, fewer course offerings, and low levels of college attendance.[33]

We need to remember that the fight for school desegregation was not simply a symbolic fight for the acknowledgment of the humanity and equality of all children. Fundamentally it was a struggle for equal access to publicly funded educational resources. Clearly that struggle continues.

CAN WE CONSIDER RACE?

It is certainly ironic that while race relations in America have changed significantly since 1954, as evidenced by the presence

15

of men and women of color in visible positions of authority and influence throughout the private and public sectors, our public schools increasingly reflect enrollment patterns reminiscent of the 1950s. In order for us to avoid further societal regression, the social implications of this enrollment pattern require our attention—for White students who are racially isolated in predominantly White schools; and for students of color who are trapped in segregated schools with limited resources.

When we consider the implications of this return to segregation for today's children, both White and of color, it is easy to feel discouraged about the future of our society. We seem to be moving backward. I recently gave a lecture on this topic, and afterward a young White woman asked me, "What can we do to change this?" I was at a loss to give a hopeful response. The window of opportunity that was created by *Brown v. Board of Education* has been closed over time by *Milliken v. Bradley, Board of Education of Oklahoma City v. Dowell,* and other court decisions. As long as we live in residentially segregated neighborhoods, it seems we will inevitably have segregated public schools. The strategy of using transportation to achieve racial balance in schools was effective in many communities, particularly in the South, but not popular among community decision-makers, as evidenced by the rapid return to neighborhood school assignments once judicial intervention was removed.

A second strategy of using "race-conscious" assignment policies at "magnet" or "exam" schools—schools with coveted special programs or innovative curricula that can attract a racially mixed group of students from across a school district—has been useful as a way to encourage voluntary integration, though because it is voluntary, the impact has not been as widespread as with forced busing. However, this approach is now also under legal attack. White parents whose children have been denied an opportunity to attend the magnet or exam school of their choice, due to the affirmative actions taken to enroll more students of color, have challenged the use of race as a criteria for selection.[34]

Consider the case of the Boston Latin School, one of three selective exam schools in the Boston public school system. Prior to 1998, admission to Boston Latin was determined using a formula based on previous grades, test scores, and race, with the goal of ensuring a racially balanced program. When a White family whose child had been denied admission made a claim of discrimination because her test scores were higher than some Black students who had been admitted, a federal court ruled that race could not be used as an admission factor. In the years since that ruling, Black and Latino enrollment at the Boston Latin School has dropped dramatically. Although Black and Latino students make up more than 75 percent of the Boston school population, they made up less than 16 percent of students enrolled at the Boston Latin School, down from 27 percent in 1998–99, the last academic year that race was used as a factor in admissions.[35]

However, in June 2003 when the Supreme Court ruled in favor of the University of Michigan Law School's consideration of race in its admission process—the case of *Grutter v. Bollinger*[36]—the Court acknowledged the compelling educational interest the law school had in maintaining a diverse student body. It recognized the extensive social science research that was submitted by the university, and in amicus briefs citing the benefits associated with greater diversity—such as increased cross-racial understanding, reduction in stereotyping, more diverse perspectives in classroom discussion, and better preparation for life and leadership in an increasingly diverse society.

The *Grutter v. Bollinger* decision, in combination with the *Gratz v. Bollinger* undergraduate admissions case,[37] clarified what was permissible for higher education admissions policies,

17

but how the Court's ruling might apply to K–12 public school assignment policies is still being determined. In *McFarland v. Jefferson County Public Schools*, the first K–12 case following the *Grutter* decision, the federal district court endorsed the consideration of race in making school assignments, in order to preserve the gains of desegregation in Jefferson County, Kentucky.[38] However, at the time this book went to press in early 2007 the Supreme Court was considering two cases focused on the constitutionality of such race-conscious school assignment policies, *Parents Involved in Community Schools v. Seattle School District No. 1* and *Meredith v. Jefferson County Board of Education et al.*

As was true in the case of *Grutter v. Bollinger*, corporate leaders and social scientists alike have filed "friend of the court" briefs in support of voluntary integration policies, highlighting the benefits to students who attend racially mixed schools and the harms incurred, particularly upon students of color, when they are confined to racially isolated schools.[39] Despite the compelling social science research in support of voluntary integration programs, Secretary of Education Margaret Spellings has advocated for the elimination of race as a criteria for assignment in public school programs.

The current composition of the Supreme Court, made more conservative by the retirement of Justice Sandra Day O'Connor in 2005 and the appointment of Justice Samuel Alito in 2006 by President George W. Bush, increases the possibility that the Court may side with the Department of Education and rule that any use of race as a selection criteria is unconstitutional. Such a ruling will undoubtedly lead to the rapid unraveling of voluntary integration plans, with few if any alternatives left to try.

One intriguing alternative was implemented in 2000 in the Wake County Public School System in North Carolina, a district that includes the capital city of Raleigh. Recognizing that race-conscious school assignments were in jeopardy, the school board decided to eliminate all references to race and ethnicity in its assignment policies, and adopted the use of school assignments on the basis of family income and student achievement level. Instead of keeping track of race in school assignments, a practice that was becoming a lightning rod for lawsuits across the country, the school board voted to limit the concentration in any school of poor students (percentage of students eligible for free and reduced lunch will be no higher than 40 percent) and of low-achieving students (percentage of students scoring below grade level should be no higher than 25 percent, averaged across a two-year period). Although initially accused of using socioeconomic status as a proxy for race, the Wake County Public School System successfully defended its new race-neutral policy, and at the same time ensured that the schools did indeed remain racially and ethnically diverse and avoided the concentration of poverty so often associated with resegregation. In the years since the 2000 decision, the achievement of low-income students has improved in both reading and math, as measured by student performance on state examinations. The apparent success of this new approach has not been without challenges, and the potential flight of middle-income parents in response to increasing low-income students in their local schools is an ongoing concern. Nevertheless, the Wake County Public School System approach is an example worthy of further study.[40]

Beyond this innovation, there seems little else to do to preserve racial diversity in schools except to encourage the residential integration of neighborhoods. However, according to a comprehensive study conducted by the Department of Housing and Urban Development (HUD) in 2000, while housing discrimination has declined generally since HUD conducted its last survey in 1989, it still persists at what the report calls "unacceptable levels" for both Black and Hispanic prospective homebuyers as well as renters, and geographic steering of Black potential homebuyers seems to be on the rise.[41] Asian Americans also experience housing discrimination, though less frequently than Blacks and Hispanics. Given this current reality, we cannot expect the composition of our neighborhoods to alter the composition of our schools anytime soon. Therefore, educators must be intentional in working to address the limitations created by racial isolation in our elementary and secondary public schools.

THE ABC APPROACH TO CREATING INCLUSIVE CLASSROOMS

What must we do? In particular, White children will need to be in schools that are intentional about helping them understand social justice issues like prejudice, discrimination, and racism, empowering them to think critically about the stereotypes to which they are exposed in the culture. Such tools will be needed to help them acquire the social skills necessary to function effectively in a diverse world. These tools will also be essential to foster continued progress in a society still struggling to disentangle the racism woven into the fabric of its founding. The hopeful news is that there are teachers, principals, and school superintendents around the country who are making the effort to create antiracist classrooms and learning environments even when their classrooms are predominantly White,[42] and there are resources available to help educators do this important work.[43]

Children of color who are in under-resourced, racially isolated schools also need such tools, as well as powerful advocates to ensure that they have committed and well-trained teachers, a challenging curriculum, and other educational resources needed to inspire their own striving for excellence. Providing these resources equitably is a daunting task, one that has never been accomplished in the history of education in the United States. The savage inequalities of school funding, so well documented by Jonathan Kozol, persist.[44] Yet we fail at our own peril. Our ability to compete in a global economy is dependent on educating all of our students—including those students of color trapped in poverty—at a high level.

We know that the problem of concentrated poverty is difficult but not impossible to overcome, as we learn of educational leaders who have fostered high levels of academic achievement despite these well-known odds. Names like Jaime Escalante and Marva Collins have become synonymous with such success—but there are many less-celebrated educators who are engaging their students and producing positive results every day. Educational researchers such as Gloria Ladson-Billings, Michele Foster, Asa Hillliard, and others have documented their success.[45]

As we learn from these and other examples, I suggest that we also need in this period to pay close attention to what I call the ABC's of creating inclusive learning environments—environments that acknowledge the continuing significance of race and racial identity in ways that can empower and motivate students to transcend the legacy of racism in our society even when the composition of their classrooms continues to reflect it. What do I mean by the ABC's? I mean *A, affirming* identity; *B, building* community; and *C, cultivating* leadership. Let me briefly expand on each of these.

A, affirming identity, refers to the fact that students need to see themselves—important dimensions of their identity—reflected in the environment around them, in the curriculum, among the faculty and staff, and in the faces of their classmates, to avoid the feelings of invisibility or marginality that can undermine student success. *B*, building community, refers to the importance of creating a school community in which everyone has a sense of belonging, a community in which there are shared norms and values as well as a sense of common purpose that unites its members. *C*, cultivating leadership, refers to the role of education in preparing citizens for active participation in a democracy, and the assumption that leadership must come from all parts of our community. Leadership in the twenty-first century requires the ability to interact effectively with people from backgrounds different from one's own—an ability that requires real-life experience.

In effective schools, all three aspects are actively attended to and developed. For instance, consider the example I witnessed at a racially mixed "magnet" school in suburban Atlanta. In 2003 I was invited there to be the speaker at a special assembly celebrating Black History Month. The principal, a White male, took obvious pride in telling me about the diversity of his school population, in which several languages are spoken and there is no clear racial majority. Cultural celebrations were common, and the Black History Month assembly was part of a series of such events held throughout the year.

Certainly for the students of African descent, this assembly was an affirmation of their presence in the school. The theme of the Black History Month assembly was "The Souls of Black Folk," in recognition of the one hundredth anniversary of the publishing of W. E. B. DuBois's classic text, a fact that in itself increased the visibility of the intellectual history of the African American community and connected the students to local history, as Professor DuBois published *The Souls of Black Folk* while teaching at Atlanta University at the beginning of the twentieth century. My presence as an author and president of Spelman College, the oldest continuing historically Black college for women, also located in Atlanta, reinforced that visibility.

Although the program was focused on the Black experience (affirming identity), a multiethnic, multiracial planning committee had worked together on the program (building community). Seated on the stage with me and the principal were the student leaders of this planning group—young men and women of all racial backgrounds—and all played a role in the program, whether introducing a speaker, reciting a poem, or giving a musical performance. The assembly began with a parade of flags representing the countries of origin of every student in the school, and with greetings in every language. Throughout the assembly it was obvious that attention had been paid to creating a program that affirmed and highlighted the history of one historically marginalized group and simultaneously reinforced the goal of building one cohesive school community.

The assembly also illustrated the third of my ABC's—cultivating leadership. Inclusive leadership takes practice. The young students who worked together to create this multicultural celebration of Black History Month were given a valuable opportunity to gain that kind of practice, and they surely learned valuable leadership lessons in the process.

The diversity of this suburban Atlanta school is clearly an asset in this example. However, every school leader needs to find ways to affirm identity, build community, and cultivate leadership within the school—even if it is racially isolated. Where do we begin? My reply must be: affirm identity. Our ability to engage our students in the kind of education they need, and that our society requires, depends on this foundational concept from which all else can flow.

AFFIRMING IDENTITY IN AN ERA OF SCHOOL DESEGREGATION

"Identities are the stories we tell ourselves and the world about who we are, and our attempt to act in accordance with these stories."[46] I love this quote, because it captures so vividly the meaning of identity. Yet before we can tell the stories ourselves, they are told to us. Our sense of identity—of self-definition— is very much shaped in childhood by what is reflected back to us by those around us. If you were asked to describe yourself using a set of adjectives, and you replied, "I am tall," "I am smart," "I am attractive," "I am outgoing," or "I am shy," whatever those descriptors might be, one might ask, "Why do you think so?" And the answer to that question might easily be, "Because that is what people have said about me. That's the feedback that I have received." Identity is shaped by the social context in which we learn about ourselves over time. Group identities—gender, race, social class, to name a few—are part of that developmental process.

When we think about identity as it is shaped in schools, one of the questions we must ask is, How do students see themselves reflected in that environment? What stories are being told about who they are? What messages are being transmitted to them in their daily interactions in classrooms and in the school hallways, and by whom? The answer today is different than it was for my parents' generation. During the school segregation of the pre-*Brown* era, Black students typically attended schools staffed by people who looked like them—educators who shared their racial and ethnic background and knew firsthand the identity stories that were being told at home and in the neighborhood. Even with inadequate school resources in impoverished communities, the shared efforts of the teachers, administrators, and families created stories of success.[47]

24

One consequence of the desegregation process in the South was the dismissal of thousands of Black teachers. When predominantly Black schools were closed and the busing of Black children began in southern school districts, Black teachers and administrators were displaced, replaced by White teachers and administrators. Active discrimination on the part of White school officials kept Black teachers out of racially mixed classrooms, particularly in the South.[48] Even very experienced teachers who had earned advanced degrees in education at such prestigious northern institutions as Teachers College at Columbia University, the University of Wisconsin, and other leading education programs in the North (which allowed Black students to enroll when southern universities did not) found themselves demoted or unemployed.[49]

Their displacement represented the rapid loss of role models, models of academic achievement, for young Black students. As doors were closing on Black teachers in the 1960s and 1970s, young African American college students interested in teaching were surely discouraged by what appeared to be declining employment opportunities. Meanwhile, doors were beginning to open in business, law, medicine, and other professions during the affirmative action years of the civil rights era. Not surprisingly, Black enrollment in teacher-education programs declined as enrollments in business administration increased.[50] The ranks of Black educators still remain well below the pre-*Brown* levels.

Indeed, of the more than 3 million teachers in the United States, only 15.6 percent are teachers of color, 7.5 percent African American, specifically. Most students of color today are being taught by a teaching force that is predominantly White and female, particularly at the elementary school level. Nowhere is the current cultural mismatch between students and teachers more visible than in urban school districts, where White women make up 65 to 76 percent (depending on grade level) of the teaching population and students of color represent 76 percent of the urban student population.[51]

Can White teachers—male or female—affirm the identities of the students of color in their classrooms? An ahistorical and idealistic response to this question might be, yes, of course. But in his essay "White Women's Work: On the Front Lines in Urban Education," Stephen Hancock reminds us that, "instead of providing students, schools and communities with better learning environments, *Brown* created (and continues to create) environments where African American and other minority students and White women teachers share dysfunctional relationships built on fear, ignorance, mistrust and resentment."[52] His description might seem harsh to some, but we cannot wish away the history of hostility that greeted Black students at school in the era of school desegregation, hostility that represented an assault on one's personhood rather than an affirmation of it. This generation of students and teachers may seem far away from that past, but its legacy lingers in the form of misinformation and stereotypes to which we are continuously exposed. If, for example, your knowledge of African American or Latino communities was based only on watching the real-life courtroom dramas so common on television today—where the frequency of people of color as plaintiffs and defendants is high—or perhaps based on a steady diet of popular music videos, what images would you hold in your mind? We carry a lifetime of these and other images with us as we interact across racial lines. How do those images shape the stories we tell students about who they are and who they will be?

Can any teacher transcend our shared history to affirm rather than assault student identities? Yes, but not without considerable effort and intention. Teachers of all backgrounds must be willing to engage in significant self-reflection about their own racial and cultural identities (a point I will return to later) to understand the assaulting stories they tell without conscious awareness. They also need to be willing to learn deeply about the lives of their students in their full cultural, socioeconomic, and sociopolitical contexts in order to affirm their identities authentically—with identity stories of hope and empowerment.

In her book *The Dreamkeepers: Successful Teachers of African American Children*, Gloria Ladson-Billings documents her classroom observations of both Black and White teachers who told such stories—teachers who worked effectively with their urban African American students, communicating high expectations and inspiring their students' best efforts. While the teachers differed in style, what they shared in common was a clear and demonstrable respect for the students and their families, and knowledge of the community from which the child came. In return they held the trust of the children and their parents.[53] Such community knowledge takes time for an outsider to acquire, and trusting relationships in a school community take time to build. One critical challenge that urban school districts face is that the teacher turnover rate in racially isolated schools with concentrated poverty is high, limiting the opportunity to gain the local knowledge needed to truly understand and then affirm the identities important to the students.[54]

We must also consider that it is not just the teachers that changed in the post-*Brown* era. The curriculum in 1954, particularly in segregated Black schools, often included some cultural dimension specific to the African American experience. Ask somebody who went to school in 1954 to recite the lines of a poem by Langston Hughes or to sing a verse of "Lift Every Voice and Sing," the James Weldon Johnson song once referred to as the "Negro National Anthem," and it is very likely that you will get a positive response. Today, if you ask a young per-

27

son of African American ancestry to do these tasks, it is more likely that he or she cannot. But what *are* the words of that song?

> Lift every voice and sing, till earth and Heaven ring,
> Ring with the harmonies of liberty;
> Let our rejoicing rise, high as the listening skies,
> Let it resound loud as the rolling sea.
> Sing a song full of the faith that the dark past has taught us,
> Sing a song full of the hope that the present has brought us;
> Facing the rising sun of our new day begun,
> Let us march on till victory is won.

> Stony the road we trod, bitter the chastening rod,
> Felt in the days when hope unborn had died;
> Yet with a steady beat, have not our weary feet,
> Come to the place for which our fathers sighed?
> We have come over a way that with tears has been watered,
> We have come, treading our path through the blood
>   of the slaughtered;
> Out from the gloomy past, till now we stand at last
> Where the White gleam of our bright star is cast.

> God of our weary years, God of our silent tears,
> Thou Who hast brought us thus far on the way;
> Thou Who hast by Thy might, led us into the light,
> Keep us forever in the path, we pray.
> Lest our feet stray from the places, our God,
>   where we met Thee.
> Lest our hearts, drunk with the wine of the world,
>   we forget Thee.
> Shadowed beneath Thy hand, may we forever stand,
> True to our God, true to our native land.[55]

There is a story about identity in those words—a story about struggle, resistance, and hope that may seem to some outdated, but that still resonates for many. What songs are our students of color singing together today?

And what difference does it make? If we think about our school environments as an illustrated book in which students look to see themselves, we have to ask, what story is being told, and who is included in the illustrations? As the environment becomes increasingly segregated, what pictures are they seeing? For young people of color in largely segregated schools, are they seeing themselves in the story, and how? They may be seeing themselves among their classmates, but they may not be seeing themselves in the curriculum in meaningful and substantive ways. In all likelihood, they are not seeing themselves among the teachers and they are not seeing themselves in the administration.

What does that mean for their own view about their possibilities, their future? Is there a relationship between invisibility in the curriculum and the underachievement of Black and Latino students? Certainly we know that motivation to learn is related to one's sense of connection to both the content and the teacher. We know that "how learners feel about the setting they are in, the respect they receive from the people around them, and their ability to trust their own thinking and experience powerfully influence their concentration, their imagination, their effort, and their willingness to continue."[56]

This point is clearly illustrated in Herbert Kohl's essay, "I Won't Learn from You."[57] He describes observing a history class being taught in a public junior high school in San Antonio, a school that served low-income Latino students but had very few Latino teachers and no Latino administrators. As the White male teacher began the day's lesson on "the first people to settle Texas" by asking students to read from the history textbook, the students demonstrated their disengagement by slumping in their seats, rolling their eyes, grimacing, and refusing to volunteer. The teacher began to read aloud the history text's account of the first settlers of Texas—pioneers from New England and the South—when one student interrupted. Knowing full well that Mexicans (his ancestors) lived in what is now known as Texas long before any New Englanders arrived, the student blurted, "What are we, animals or something?" The teacher, ignoring his student's point completely, replied, "What does that have to do with the text?" In apparent frustration, the teacher left the room, leaving his visitor, Herbert Kohl, in charge of the class. Kohl reread the passage from the text and asked the students whether they believed what they had just heard. His question captured their attention, and he continued, saying, "This is lies, nonsense. In fact, I think the textbook is racist and an insult to everyone in this room." Kohl's response to the text opened the door for an important dialogue. He writes:

> The class launched into a serious and sophisticated discussion of the way in which racism manifests itself in their everyday lives at school. And they described the stance they took in order to resist that racism and yet not be thrown out of school. It amounted to nothing less than full-blown and cooperative not-learning. They accepted the failing grades it produced in exchange for the passive defense of their personal and cultural integrity. This was a class of school failures, and perhaps, I believed then and still believe, the repository for the positive leadership and intelligence of their generation.[58]

Kohl captures the essence of their resistance in this conclusion: "To agree to learn from a stranger who does not respect your integrity"—or as I would say, your identity—"causes a major loss of self. The only alternative is to not-learn and reject their world." As the noted theorist Jean Baker Miller once said, we all want to feel "seen, heard, and understood."[59] At its core, that is what affirming identity means. It is not just about what pictures are hanging on the wall, or what content is included in the curriculum, though these things are important. It is about recognizing students' lives—and helping them make connections to them. In Kohl's example, the State of Texas or the local school district may have required that the teacher use that particular history text, but the conversation was not scripted. It was Kohl's willingness to acknowledge the contradiction between the students' lives and the text that affirmed them and engaged them.

Affirming identity is not just about being nice—it is about being knowledgeable about who our students are, and reflecting a story that resonates with their best hope for themselves. This distinction is aptly captured by Mary Ginley, a teacher, who writes:

> A warm friendly teacher is nice but it isn't enough. We have plenty of warm friendly teachers who tell the kids nicely to forget their Spanish and ask mommy and daddy to speak to them in English at home; who give them easier tasks so they won't feel badly when the work becomes difficult; who never learn about what life is like at home or what they eat or what music they like or what stories they have been told or what their history is. Instead we smile and give them a hug and tell them to eat our food and listen to our stories and dance to our music. We teach them to read with our words and wonder why it's so hard for them. We ask them to sit quietly and we'll tell them what's important and what they must know to "get ready for the next grade." And we never ask them who they are and where they want to go.[60]

Affirming identity is about asking who they are, and where they want to go, and conveying a fundamental belief that they can get there—through the development of their intellect and their critical capacity to think. Any teacher—White or of color —willing to work at affirming identity will have engaged students.

However, the task of creating identity stories is not that of the school alone. Of course the messages we receive at home from family and friends from the time of our birth are powerful parts of our narrative as well—for better or worse. But as educators we must acknowledge the impact of the many hours spent in school and the influence even one teacher can have on the story a student tells him or herself—also for better or worse. We cannot control the stories others are telling—but we must take responsibility for the identity stories we tell.

The community network of adults can help build that narrative as well. For example, I was recently invited to speak to a group of African American high school students who were part of an Atlanta-based organization called the W. E. B. DuBois Society in Atlanta. The students in the W. E. B. DuBois Society voluntarily come together on Saturday mornings to hear speakers and to discuss ideas in a context that affirms their shared cultural heritage. Collectively they are told a story about the legacy of academic achievement of which they are a part. In preparation for my visit, they had all read my 1997 book about the experience of race in predominantly White schools, and they came with copies in hand, ready to ask me some very well-prepared questions. These students shared in common the experience of being in independent schools or suburban public schools where they were in the minority. On that particular occasion, they were joined by the principal of one of the schools represented who was also interested in hearing my presentation. While the W. E. B. DuBois Society was not an organization under the direction of the principal, his presence clearly symbolized the school's support for the students' participation.

The image of these young teenagers voluntarily spending a Saturday morning focused on academic content runs directly counter to how many people ordinarily define Black adolescent popular culture and activity. But the adults in their environment have created a space for them to come together that clearly affirms their shared sense of identity in positive ways, helping them to tell a story about themselves as young scholars capable of high academic achievement, and they have responded with enthusiasm. We all want a good story to tell about ourselves. We have to provide historically marginalized youth with the information and feedback to help construct that story and then celebrate them when they do.

What about affirming the identities of White children? White children in a largely White school environment typically see themselves in the curriculum. They learn about White authors, scientists, inventors, artists, and explorers—most often male, but not exclusively so. The opportunity to envision oneself in similar roles is regularly offered to White children through the example of White adults. While certainly there is ethnic variation, socioeconomic variation, and religious variation that mediates the ease with which a child might identify with such examples, it is still likely that there will be places where White students see themselves reflected, at least in the faces of their teachers and their administrators—the adults they arguably observe most closely doing their jobs in the larger world for the most extended period of time—a privilege that students of color cannot take for granted. While the individual narratives they are constructing in childhood will vary with family circumstance and personal characteristics, as they do for all of us, the group story of what it means to be White is a story of achievement, success, and of being in charge.

But how do White children see *others* reflected? Are they learning about people of color as equals or does the curriculum continue to reinforce old notions of assumed White superiority as the result of unchallenged stereotypes and unrecognized omissions of information about the societal contributions of people of color? Are they receiving information that will help them navigate a global society, information that will help them engage with people who are different from themselves in that environment? In the absence of such information, the story is incomplete and they are not well served by their education.

For more than twenty years I taught a course on the psychology of racism, in the context of predominantly White institutions. The students in my class, most of whom were White, would often express anger and a sense of betrayal when they discovered new information about the social history of race relations in this country that they had never learned in their K–12 education. "Why didn't anyone tell us this before?" they would ask.[61] Having the information helped them understand the context for their cross-racial interactions, and it helped them see how they could be active agents for change within their own spheres of influence, knowledge that was empowering for them. The sanitized versions of U.S. history that distort reality (as in "the first settlers of Texas" in our earlier example) and obliterate the presence of so many—men and women of color who shaped and participated in the making of science, art, literature, the economy, in short, the fabric of our society—leave White children at risk for the arrogance that comes from ignorance, and unable to make useful sense of the world around them.[62]

Consider this conversation between two White women in the days following the news coverage of the flooding of New Orleans in the aftermath of Hurricane Katrina in 2005. Frances Kendall, author of *Understanding White Privilege,* writes: "One of my family members said to me, 'Weren't the White people smart to buy their houses on higher ground?' Her unexamined belief system was that everyone had the same real estate opportunities and the White people just *happened* to make the right decisions."[63] How was it that she did not know about the long history of housing discrimination, racial covenants, and the economic deprivation associated with slavery and legalized segregation that placed Black neighborhoods below sea level in New Orleans? Kendall explains:

> For some of us, there is extreme pain in looking at what was done to others by our ancestors in order to retain privileged positions. We would rather ignore it or call it something else, for example seeing slavery as an "economic" rather than a racial issue or viewing the taking of the West as simply our "frontier" spirit. We rationalize these acts as necessary for the health and strength of "our" nation. If we see ourselves as White, we have to deal with the guilt, shame, and confusion that comes as we think of the treatment of African Americans, Latinos, American Indians, Japanese Americans, and so forth.[64]

Given the discomfort associated with this history, it is not surprising that teachers might avoid talking about it. But there is an alternative to silence and misrepresentation that can affirm the identities of White children as well as build capacity for connection across racial lines in the future. If we were given a full understanding of our past and present, we would learn about the cross-racial coalitions that were built at every period of progress in our history. We would learn about the courage, cooperation, and perseverance demonstrated by Whites in alliance with people of color in response to social injustice.

There is an institution in Cincinnati that exemplifies this

vision of education. The National Underground Railroad Freedom Center was created there on the banks of the Ohio River to preserve not only the memory of the history of cross-racial cooperation when White abolitionists helped determined Africans escape from the bondage of White slave owners, but to also call attention to contemporary struggles for justice and freedom around the world where people of different backgrounds have worked together to bring about change. This is the history that every child in America needs to learn, but it is especially important for White children, in order for them to be able to acknowledge their Whiteness—a social identity that still has meaning in our society—with a story that is a source of pride, rather than shame or guilt.

In a race-conscious society, the development of a positive sense of racial or ethnic identity, not based on assumed superiority or inferiority, is an important task for everyone. It is an important task for people of color. It is an important task for White people. Sometimes when people hear the phrase "White identity," what comes to mind are connotations of White supremacy, as embodied by the Ku Klux Klan, perhaps. But of course the notion of White identity relevant here is not one based on a sense of assumed superiority. What is necessary, rather, is recognition of the meaning of Whiteness in our society. As many scholars and writers have explored in recent years, Whiteness is not an identity without meaning. Some White people who haven't thought much about these issues will say, "Well, you know, I'm an individual. I want you to see me as an individual." And of course, each of us is an individual, and we want our individuality recognized. But we each also have a social identity, with a social history, a social meaning. Recognition of the meaning of Whiteness in our society is recognition of the meaning of *privilege* in the context of a society that advantages being White.

Now, urging White teachers and students to recognize the meaning of their Whiteness is *not* equivalent to asking them to feel guilty about their privilege, although sometimes guilt *is* part of that exploration of identity for many people. Feeling badly about one's own Whiteness is a stage that many people experience.[65] It's certainly not the goal of the educational process nor should it be the end point. Ideally, we should each be able to embrace all of who we are, and to recognize that in a society where race is still meaningful and where Whiteness is still a source of power and privilege, that it is possible to resist being in the role of dominator, or "oppressor," and to become genuinely antiracist in one's White identity, and to actively work against systems of injustice and unearned privilege. It is possible to claim both one's Whiteness as a part of who one is and of one's daily experience, and the identity of being what I like to call a "White ally": namely, a White person who understands that it is possible to use one's privilege to create more equitable systems; that there are White people throughout history who have done exactly that; and that one can align oneself with that history. That is the identity story that we have to reflect to White children, and help them see themselves in it in order to continue the racial progress in our society.

When White adults have not thought about their own racial identity, it is difficult for them to respond to the identity-development needs of either White children or children of color. Consequently, it becomes very important to engage teachers around these issues in pre-service preparation and in ongoing professional development. The intergenerational transmission of incomplete and distorted identity stories is a problem that we must address at the level of teacher preparation—and for the thousands of teachers already in the classroom, as part of ongoing professional development, a conversation that I will elaborate on in Chapter 2. The need is particularly pressing for

White teachers, who represent the vast majority of the public school educators in the United States, but it applies to all teachers. We cannot assume that teachers of color are confident in their abilities to talk about these issues as well. None of us can teach what we haven't learned ourselves. The good news is that those who have engaged in a process of examining their own racial or ethnic identity, and who feel affirmed in it, are more likely to be respectful of the self-definition that others claim, and are much more effective working in multiracial settings. It is these members of our society who can help us move beyond the regressive state of our current educational system, and move us forward into the twenty-first century with hope.

TWO

Connecting the Dots

How Race in America's
Classrooms Affects Achievement

As part of a program sponsored by the National Staff Development Council, an organization committed to ensuring success for all students through staff development and school improvement, I had the opportunity to dialogue with colleagues from around the country about some of the challenges associated with what I call antiracist professional development for educators. One man expressed his frustration that many school districts only wanted to talk about closing the "achievement gap," usually defined as a disparity in school performance between White students and students of color (particularly Black and Latino students) as evidenced by standardized test scores and overall grade point averages. The decision makers he described did not want to invest resources of time or money in any larger conversations about race in schools. How, he asked, could he persuade them to support antiracist professional development?

I replied: You have to help them see how unexamined racial attitudes can negatively impact student performance, and how a willingness to break the silence about the impact of race in schools as part of a program of antiracist professional development can improve achievement. *You have to connect the dots.* At a time when America is fixated myopically on test-score disparities yet making little progress on eliminating them, we all need to see the connections between notions of race and intelligence in America's classrooms, the academic achievement of underperforming students of color, and the benefit of antiracist professional development. Connecting those dots is my project in this chapter.

We must always begin by acknowledging the social and historical context in which we operate. That context shapes in powerful ways how we think and act. One important dimension of that context is the fact that American schools were never designed to educate everyone. We often talk about the importance of an educated citizenry for a successful democracy, and I certainly agree that such a citizenry is necessary. However, when our democracy was being established, only White male landowners could vote. The educated citizenry that our founding fathers had in mind did not include many of the people who will read this essay. White women were not allowed to vote until 1920. The Constitution originally defined enslaved Africans as equivalent to three-fifths of a person without the rights of citizenship, and in slaveholding states it was illegal to educate them. The right to vote was hard-won, and not guaranteed for African Americans until the Voting Rights Act of 1965, less than a lifetime ago. As I have argued, the history of desegregation of the public schools during the 1960s and 1970s and the subsequent resegregation of schools in the 1980s and 1990s following key Supreme Court decisions make evident that race still matters in schools.[1] From the beginning, American constructions of race and class have determined who had access to education, and to a large degree those constructions still shape how we think about who can benefit from it.

Additionally, American constructions of intelligence, closely interwoven with our notions of race and class, have shaped how we think about who can benefit from education. Historically, our schools have been structured to identify those with high potential and those without, and to sort them accordingly. Fundamentally, that is the purpose of ability grouping, also known as tracking, a well-established practice in schools across the country. Although today I often hear educators and politicians alike emphasize the idea that all children can and must learn at a high level, I sometimes wonder if they really believe their own rhetoric. If they do, such thinking represents a recent shift in ideology that still is not reflected in the organizational structure of most schools. Tracking persists. The technological demands of the information age make greater levels of academic achievement and postsecondary education a necessity, but our schools still reflect the assumptions of the industrial age, when the majority of students were expected to enter the world of work performing routinized tasks, rather than pursue advanced education and professions requiring critical analysis or creative thinking. The idea of widespread access to a college education is a relatively new concept in our society, and we have never provided the necessary preparation in a widespread way. No wonder we find it hard to do now.

If we are really serious about creating learning environments that foster high levels of achievement for all of our students, irrespective of race and class, we have to examine and challenge a fundamental notion central to the educational process—the notion of intelligence. The concept of intelligence as an inborn attribute that determines one's capacity to learn is an idea firmly embedded in our society and our educational system.[2] And who can question that some people seem to process information faster than others? We see evidence of that all around us, every day. I do not question that there may be individual variation in the speed of our neural synapses. The ques-

41

tion we might ask is, How fast is fast enough? The social psychologist and educator Jeff Howard has argued that if you have learned to speak your native language by the age of three (a task of considerable cognitive complexity), then you have all the synaptic speed you need to be successful in school. The key to your success in school is not inborn ability, but rather effective effort produced in the context of high expectations.[3] But this idea that most of us are *smart enough* to achieve at a high level in school runs counter to our long-standing practice of testing and sorting. So where did the idea of testing and sorting come from—and what does it have to do with race?

THE AMERICAN INVENTION OF INTELLIGENCE AND THE POWER OF EXPECTATIONS

To answer that question, we need to go back to the introduction of the idea of intelligence as something that could be quantified and measured using standardized tests. Alfred Binet, a French psychologist, is credited with inventing the first intelligence test in 1905, though that was not his stated intention. He was commissioned by the French minister of public education to develop techniques for identifying children who might need special educational services. The test he created was intended to be administered individually, and he was very specific about how his new measure should be used. He believed that intelligence was too multidimensional to capture with a single number or score, and he worried that the use of his test would lead to inappropriate labeling of children. Binet insisted that the test he created should *not* be used as a general device for ranking all students—but should only be used for the *limited* purpose of identifying children whose poor performance might indicate a need for special education, those who today might be classified as mildly retarded or perhaps having specific learning disabilities. The aim of testing, he said, should be to identify children in order to help them improve, not to place labels on them which in themselves could become limiting.[4]

However, as Stephen Jay Gould documents in his classic text, *The Mismeasure of Man,* all of Binet's caveats were disregarded when his test was imported to America. The misuse of his and other tests was fueled by two ideas that were actively embraced by leading American psychologists in the early twentieth century. The first is the idea of reification—the assumption that test scores represent a single, measurable characteristic of brain functioning called general intelligence. The second is the idea of hereditarianism, the assumption that intelligence, as measured by tests, is largely inherited, and thus independent of major environmental differences between racial and ethnic groups in our society. Perhaps not surprisingly, the hereditarian theory of intelligence grew in popularity in America at a time of extreme nationalism during the early twentieth century, a time when a wave of immigration from southern and eastern Europe was taking place. Two prominent psychologists, Henry Herbert Goddard and Lewis M. Terman, played pivotal roles in the spread of these ideas.[5]

Goddard is sometimes called the father of intelligence testing because he first translated Binet's test into English and introduced it into the United States. His interest was inspired by his work as the director of an institution in New Jersey called the Vineland Training School for Feeble-Minded Girls and Boys. He enjoyed his work with the students there and became very interested in both the causes of mental deficiency and the teaching methods employed by the instructors. His research facility at the school has been described as the first laboratory for the scientific study of mentally retarded persons. In Goddard's day, there were three categories of mental deficiency: idiots, imbeciles, and feeble-minded.

Idiots and imbeciles (language considered offensive today) were what we would now identify as severely or moderately retarded individuals. Those who could not develop full speech and had a mental age below three were considered idiots, and those with a mental age between three and seven who could not master written language were considered imbeciles, categories relatively easy to identify. Goddard's interest in testing was sparked by his concern about identifying those who were what he called "high-grade defectives" or "morons," people who could function in society but who were "feeble-minded." In his view, such people were a menace because they threatened to weaken the gene pool of American intelligence.[6]

Goddard was the first popularizer of the Binet test in America; he believed that the test was perfect for identifying the feeble-minded, but unlike Binet, his goal was not to help these individuals perform better in school. Goddard considered the test scores as measures of a single, innate entity, and his goal was to identify the mentally deficient, then segregate them and keep them from having children, in order to prevent the demise of American society. Clearly he was a believer in eugenics, though he acknowledged that widespread sterilization of people of low intelligence was impractical.[7] He was not alone in his concern about the threat that such individuals posed, however.

By the end of the nineteenth century, American concern about immigration was growing, fueled by fears that a large percentage of the new arrivals were mentally deficient. In 1882 the United States Congress passed a law prohibiting people believed to be mentally defective from passing through the Ellis Island checkpoint. Enforcing this law proved to be difficult, because as many as five thousand immigrants needed to be inspected each day. In 1910 Goddard was among those invited to Ellis Island to investigate how the screening process might be expedited. In 1912 he returned to the island, accompanied by two specially trained assistants. The procedure he developed was a two-step process. One assistant would visually screen for suspected mental defectives as the immigrants passed through the checkpoint. These individuals would then proceed to another location, where the other assistant would assess them with a variety of performance measures and a revised version of the Binet test. Goddard believed that trained inspectors could be more accurate than the Ellis Island physicians; the key to their success was expertise developed through experience.[8] In 1913 Goddard wrote:

> After a person has had considerable experience in this work, he almost gets a sense of what a feeble-minded person is so that he can tell one afar off. The people who are best at this work, and who I believe should do this work, are women. Women seem to have closer observation than men. It was quite impossible for others to see how these two young women could pick out the feeble-minded without the aid of the Binet test at all.[9]

Among those tested according to the procedures utilized by Goddard and his staff in 1912, 83 percent of the Jews, 80 percent of the Hungarians, 79 percent of the Italians, and 87 percent of the Russians were identified as "feeble-minded." The number of immigrants who were deported increased dramatically as a result of Goddard's new screening measures.[10]

Even Goddard was surprised that these percentages were so high, but the data did not lead him—as it should have—to conclude that there was a problem with his assessment procedure. He resolved, instead, that the United States was now scraping the bottom of the barrel as far as the immigrant populations were concerned. In 1917 he wrote, "We cannot escape the general conclusion that these immigrants were of surprisingly low intelligence.... We are now getting the poorest of each race."[11]

However, by 1928 Goddard had changed his mind about the value of those individuals that his procedures had determined were of limited intelligence. He wrote: "They do a great deal of work that no one else will do.... There is an immense amount of drudgery to be done, an immense amount of work for which we do not wish to pay enough to secure more intelligent workers.... May it be that possibly the moron has his place."[12]

Although Goddard is credited with bringing Binet's scale to America, it was Lewis Terman, a Stanford University professor, who brought it to American schools. Terman revised the test to create the Stanford-Binet Intelligence Scale. The test as standardized by Terman led to the simplification of test results represented by a single number, a number we commonly refer to as IQ, or intelligence quotient. A score of 100 was established as the norm for "average" children.[13] Like Goddard, Terman was an influential psychologist, and he had strongly held views about the fixed and unchanging quality of intelligence as an inherited characteristic. He was also an advocate of eugenics, and he expressed his views on the subject in a widely used textbook, published in 1916, titled *The Measurement of Intelligence*.[14] He shared Goddard's concerns about the negative impact on society by the "feeble-minded." Terman wrote:

> Among laboring men and servant girls there are thousands like them. They are the world's "hewers of wood and drawers of water." And yet, as far as intelligence is concerned, the tests have told the truth.... No amount of school instruction will ever make them intelligent voters or capable citizens in the true sense of the word.... The fact that one meets this type

with such frequency among Indians, Mexicans, and [N]egroes suggests quite forcibly that the whole question of racial differences in mental traits will have to be taken up anew and by experimental methods.... Children of this group should be segregated in special classes and be given instruction which is concrete and practical. They cannot master abstractions, but they can often be made efficient workers, able to look out for themselves. There is no possibility at present of convincing society that they should not be allowed to reproduce, although from a eugenic point of view they constitute a grave problem because of their unusually prolific breeding.[15]

Although these ideas sound sinister today, these were mainstream writers and thinkers who enjoyed considerable influence in the American educational system. The Stanford-Binet test led to widespread testing in American schools, and the results were used to sort students according to their measured ability. Terman's test gave U.S. educators the first simple, quick, cheap, and seemingly objective way to "track" students, or assign them to different course sequences according to their perceived ability.

The notion of intelligence testing was further popularized during World War I, when Robert Yerkes developed the Army mental tests, the first mass-administered intelligence test, used to screen U.S. Army recruits and determine appropriate assignments. The test was given to 1.75 million recruits.[16] Like Goddard and Terman, Yerkes believed that IQ was genetically determined, even though his data suggested otherwise. For example, he continually found a relationship between performance on the intelligence tests and the amount of schooling a recruit had had. Yet Yerkes did not conclude that schooling leads to increased scores; rather, he argued that men with more innate intelligence spend more time in school. When Blacks from the North did better on the tests than southern Whites, he did not conclude that the result had to do with better access to education in the North (where education funding was much higher than in the South)—instead he argued that only the most intelligent Blacks had managed to move North. When immigrant populations did better on the tests the longer they had been in the country, he and other hereditarians did not conclude that this was the result of new learning, but that the more recent immigrants (largely from southern and eastern Europe) came from a more deficient gene pool than those who had come earlier (primarily English and northern European immigrants).[17]

The Army data, combined with ethnocentrism, resulted in the 1924 Restriction Act to limit immigration from southern and eastern Europe. Today we can see that the "hereditarian bias" of Terman, Goddard, Yerkes, and others blinded these researchers to interpretations of their data that made more sense than the ones they relied upon.

Today, most researchers acknowledge that heredity is one factor influencing intelligence—just as heredity influences height. But environmental factors like poor nutrition ultimately impact how tall you are (whatever your genetic makeup). It seems obvious that intelligence, which is even more multiply determined than a characteristic like height, is also impacted by environmental influences both in and out of school. Most psychologists today certainly believe this to be the case. And yet the influence of Goddard, Terman, and Yerkes—eminent psychologists in their day—continues to be felt today in the assumptions that most people make about what it is that intelligence tests are measuring, and the role of heredity in determining school success.

Hereditarian assumptions are only one problem with the American understanding of intelligence. Reification is another

—the idea that test scores represent a single thing in the head called "general intelligence" that can be measured by a single number. With the invention of factor analysis (a statistical procedure) in 1904 by Charles Spearman, "g" (general intelligence) was born. By taking multiple scores and manipulating them mathematically through the process known as factor analysis, you can get a single number that expresses a relationship (correlation) between the scores used. That number is called a factor. A factor is not a thing or a cause, it is a mathematical abstraction. And it is not the only mathematical conclusion possible, it is only one of the ways one might analyze data. Spearman, however, was convinced that through this process of factor analysis he had identified a single, measurable entity called intelligence.[18]

Spearman's "g" was an important cornerstone in the arguments of the hereditarians. In 1937 Sir Cyril Burt, the official psychologist of the London public schools, joined the two concepts when he wrote, "This general intellectual factor, central and all-pervading, shows a further characteristic, also disclosed by testing and statistics. It appears to be inherited, or at least inborn. Neither knowledge nor practice, neither interest nor industry, will avail to increase it."[19] Burt's name is an important one in this story, because he published influential studies of identical twins raised apart. If intelligence is determined by heredity rather than environment, then identical twins raised in different environments should still have very similar IQ scores.

Burt provided data that demonstrated just that. However, after his death in 1976, it was discovered that, in one of the great intellectual hoaxes of the century, *Burt had fabricated his data*— it was totally unreliable. His fabrications are now believed to have begun in the 1940s, after his real data was destroyed during the London blitz. However, Gould, in his in-depth review of Burt's scholarly writing, concludes that Burt's work was flawed from the onset because of his inability to view his own data with reasonable objectivity. "Burt's hereditarian argument had no foundation in his empirical work (either honest or fraudulent)... it represented an a priori bias, imposed upon the studies that supposedly proved it. It also acted, through Burt's zealous pursuit of his idée fixe, as a distorter of judgment and finally as an incitement to fraud."[20] But the fraud went undiscovered until after his death, and Burt was still publishing his articles in prestigious psychological journals as late as 1972.

Heir to Burt's flawed intellectual legacy, Arthur Jensen wrote a controversial article published in 1969 in the *Harvard Educational Review,* in which he argued against compensatory education programs like Head Start, claiming that IQ was an inherited, fixed ability, unable to be changed by early intervention.[21] Jensen based most of his argument on Burt's data, the same data that was later discredited. A generation later, in 1994, Richard J. Herrnstein and Charles Murray published *The Bell Curve,* making essentially the same arguments that Jensen made, rooted in the intellectual history of Goddard, Terman, and Yerkes.[22]

What do all of these scholars have in common, besides what we might call "bad science"? The first group was working in the early 1920s, at the height of an influx of immigrants who were different from the Anglo-Saxon Protestants who had preceded them, many of whom were politically radical and supportive of labor unions.[23] Jensen was writing at the height of the civil rights movement. *The Bell Curve* authors published their book during a time of economic slowdown, concern about jobs, and growing unease among many White people about affirmative action policies. All represent a backlash against progressive movements—essentially arguing for support of the status quo, using a hereditarian argument. In essence, they argue, why change social and educational policies if the outcome is ultimately determined by our biology?

What alternatives are there to these problematic views of intelligence? The psychologist Howard Gardner is well known for his views of multiple intelligences (not just a single g factor).[24] But even before Gardner, there was Jean Piaget, the Swiss developmental psychologist who defined intelligence as an ongoing process of adaptation, not a fixed trait. Piaget understood intelligence as cognitive capacity that develops as a result of individuals' active engagement with their environment, capacity that gets more complex over time as the result of individual experience.[25] This idea is echoed in the work of Jeff Howard, who talks about "smart" as something someone becomes through effective effort, not an unchanging characteristic.[26]

It is worth reviewing the history of notions of intelligence in our effort to connect the dots of race and achievement, because I think it essential to understand both how deeply embedded a scientifically suspect idea is in our American system of education, and how inherently rooted in the racism of the eugenics movement it is.

Combine this with the long tradition of stereotypical representations of Black and Latino people in popular culture as either stupid, lazy, dangerous, hypersexual, or all of those things combined, and we have a situation in which it is very likely that Black and Latino children will enter school situations in which they are disadvantaged from the beginning by a teacher's lowered expectations as compared to those he or she may have for the White students in the class.

This is a crucial point. I am not saying that most or many teachers are actively, consciously racist in their belief system (though of course some are). But we are all products of our culture and its history. Regardless of our own racial or ethnic backgrounds, we have all been exposed to racial stereotypes and flawed educational psychology, and unless we are consciously working to counter their influence on our behavior, it is likely that they will shape (subtly perhaps) our interactions with those who have been so stereotyped. To prevent this outcome, we need active intervention in the form of antiracist education and professional development.

The importance of teacher expectations should not be underestimated. Many readers will be familiar with the classic study conducted by Robert Rosenthal and Lenore Jacobson, testing the impact of teacher expectations on student performance.[27] All of the children in the study were administered a nonverbal test of intelligence, which was disguised as a test that would predict intellectual development, or "blooming."

Approximately 20 percent of the children were chosen at random to form the experimental group. The teachers of these children were told that their scores on the test indicated that they would show surprising gains in intellectual competence during the next eight months of school. The only difference between the children in the experimental group and those in the control group was what their teachers had been told about them. At the end of the school year, eight months later, all of the children were retested with the same nonverbal measure. Overall, the children who had been identified as bloomers had done just that. They showed a significantly greater gain, known as the Pygmalion effect, than did the children of the control group. The children had risen to meet the expectations of the teacher.[28]

This study, and variations of it, have been replicated many times since it was first conducted in 1966, and researchers, now convinced of the power of expectations, have shifted their focus to how the teacher's expectation is communicated. One finding that has emerged is that teachers appear to teach more content and to teach it with more warmth of affect to children for whom they have high expectations.[29]

A teacher's affect and expectations can be communicated in many ways. In an interview I conducted as part of a research project on identity development among Black college students, a young Black woman taking an introductory science course at a prestigious, predominantly White institution reported her effort to seek extra help after doing poorly on an exam. When she appeared at the professor's office door during his stated office hours, he was meeting with a young White man, in what appeared to her to be a friendly and helpful conversation. She waited her turn outside his door, but when she entered his office and began to explain her confusion, he replied, "I can't help you." What did he mean? Was he saying, "I can't help you now, this is an inconvenient time," or did he mean, "I can't help you, you are beyond my help"? While either interpretation is a possibility, the student read his tone of voice and body language as dismissive, in contrast to what she had observed with the student before her, and interpreted his statement to mean the latter. She left his office, hurt and disappointed, only to continue to flounder in his course.

The message does not have to be so directly communicated to have a negative impact. Everyday interactions send an important message as well. Does the teacher offer a genuine smile when you enter the room? Does he or she greet you by name (and make the effort to pronounce it correctly)? Do you get called on in class when you raise your hand? If you offer a wrong or incomplete answer, does the teacher prompt you to try again or expand your response?

When my children were growing up, we would often visit local museums and attend the interactive demonstrations designed for children. When the museum staff person would ask the gathered group of children a question, my oldest son would always raise his hand energetically to reply. Inevitably, someone else, almost always a White child, would be called on. While I realize that the small number of Black children typically present in the crowd meant that the odds were always in favor of a White child being called on, what was disheartening to me was my observation that after a while my son stopped raising his hand. What was an occasional experience at the museum for him is a daily experience for some children in classrooms where teacher behavior may be influenced by unexamined biases. Creating an opportunity to examine such biases through professional development can lead to changes in these everyday behaviors.

For example, after participating in a semester-long antiracist professional development course I developed, in which teachers were actively encouraged to examine their own racial socialization and the ways in which stereotypes impacted their classroom practice, the educators involved, most of whom were White, reported new actions they had taken to reach out to students of color and engage their parents in the learning process, often for the first time.[30] One such educator offered this example:

> My thinking throughout this course...prompted me to call Dwight at home one night just to see if he was doing his homework and to let him know that I was thinking about him and wondering if he needed help on the math problems. He was shocked that I called but I could tell that he was pleased to get the special treatment. Dwight has been a different student since that phone call. Things are far from perfect, but in general he's doing much better.[31]

Reaching out to this student communicated in a new and tangible way this teacher's genuine concern and belief that her student was capable of succeeding.

Ironically, sometimes low expectations can be hidden behind an ostensibly positive response from a teacher, in the form of inflated grades. I recall a particular instance of working with an African American student when I was teaching at a predominantly White institution in New England. She was an older first-generation college student who had overcome many hardships to be in college. She was an enthusiastic participant in class discussion, who often made positive contributions to our dialogue. But when the student turned in a poorly written paper, I gave her a C on it. I knew she aspired to earn a PhD in psychology, and in my written feedback to her, I suggested that she work on her writing skills, not only to improve her performance in my class but to be better-prepared for graduate school. My intention was to encourage her, conveying both my own high standard and my confidence in her capacity to improve her writing with assistance and effort.

Despite my good intentions, she was upset with me and came to talk to me about her grade and my comments. My suggestion that she needed help with her writing was especially unsettling for her. "I just did a paper for another class and got an A on it," she said. *How is that possible?* I thought to myself, given the quality of the writing I had seen. I knew the White male professor who had given her the A pretty well, and I felt comfortable enough in my relationship with him to call him up after the student left my office. I explained the situation and my puzzlement about the disparity in our grading of her written work. He agreed with my assessment that her writing skills were weak, but then elaborated on the many disadvantages she had overcome to be in college, and in conclusion said, "You know, she works really hard." He had in essence given her an A for effort.

As our conversation continued, he spoke candidly about his reluctance to penalize the student for the inadequacy of her segregated urban high school preparation, and his desire not to be perceived as racially biased in his grading. I talked to him about my perception of the inherent racism in his essentially condescending—though well intentioned—awarding of a high grade. If he ordinarily gave honest feedback to more-privileged White students, to deny a Black student similarly honest feedback was to disadvantage her further. I argued that without honest feedback or high standards, without the demand for excellence, this student would not be able to accomplish what she wanted to accomplish. His high grade was in a real way an expression of *low expectations*, revealing a lack of confidence in her capacity to improve her skills with focused effort.

I never told the student about my conversation with the other professor. But her writing in my class did start to show improvement. And she did eventually go on to graduate school. Neither the conversation with the student or the professor was particularly easy to have—but both were important to me. It felt necessary for me to convey my high expectations to my student, and as it turned out, also to my colleague. In the end, I think they both appreciated it.

Just as low expectations can prevent honest and constructive feedback in the face of poor performance, they can also prevent the recognition of excellent performance from those from which little has been expected. Consider the example of Gwendolyn Parker, a Harvard graduate and writer, who as a child loved to write poetry. When given the task of writing a poem for a class assignment in high school, she did her very best and expected to receive an A. Instead she received a C- and was brave enough to ask the teacher about the low grade. His response clearly conveyed his expectations: "There is no way that you could have written this poem. . . . I searched all weekend, looking for where you may have copied it from. . . . If I'd been able to find out where you plagiarized it from, I would have given you an F. But since I couldn't find it, you are lucky I gave you a C-."[32]

The teacher was clearly angry, perhaps not just because he suspected cheating but because his assumptions of his student's intellectual inferiority were being so blatantly challenged. Regrettably, Parker's recollection is not the only such account that I have heard. Throughout my teaching career in predominantly White institutions, Black students have shared examples of instances where their competence and integrity have been questioned when their schoolwork exceeded the expectations of their teachers. As with Goddard, Terman, Yerkes, and Burt, subjective bias prevented the teachers from making the correct interpretation of the data before them—the excellence of the work.

Commenting on Parker's experience and those of young people like her whose parents had migrated to the North to escape the Jim Crow segregation of the South, Theresa Perry wrote: "If in the South the struggle was for equal facilities, equal pay for teachers, classroom buildings, a local high school and materials, in the North the struggle would be against the assumption—no, the ideology—of Black children as intellectually inferior and against school assignments, assessments, and interactions based on this ideology."[33] Such an ideology was reinforced in the popular culture and, as we have seen, in the scholarly literature. No wonder it infused the schools. Without intentional activity to shift the paradigm, it is easily perpetuated from one generation of teachers to the next.

THE PSYCHOLOGICAL THREAT OF STEREOTYPES

Well-entrenched assumptions about intelligence and racial and ethnic stereotypes do not just influence teacher behavior. They also impact student behavior over the years of their schooling. Particularly during adolescence, students who have internalized the negative messages about their own group are at risk for manifesting those stereotypes in school when they begin actively trying to define their own sense of racial/ethnic identity. Some African American students may have come to believe that high academic achievement in school is territory reserved for White students. Certainly the curriculum, devoid of Black role models, and the demographics of the tracking pattern in many schools, heavily skewed in favor of White students, would support that conclusion. Some African American students may actively choose to distance themselves from "White" behaviors, meanwhile embracing "Black" behaviors as defined by the popular culture as an expression of "authentic Blackness," for example, behaviors that may run counter to school success. It should be noted that concern about "acting White" is not a universal phenomenon among Black adolescents. However, in those environments where it seems common, one must ask what factors have led to the internalization of those beliefs among Black students. Perry poses the essence of this question: "What are the institutional formations and ideologies of teachers and schools that construct and reproduce these beliefs about schooling?"[34] It is a question that every teacher and administrator who has heard the phrase "acting White" used by Black children must ask.

The social psychologist Claude Steele and his colleagues have identified another way that awareness of the assumption of intellectual inferiority can impact Black students, and that is the phenomenon of "stereotype threat." As defined by Steele, stereotype threat is "the threat of being viewed through the lens of a negative stereotype, or the fear of doing something that would inadvertently confirm that stereotype."[35] The studies that demonstrate this effect are elegantly designed and convincingly clear. For example, in one of their experiments, the researchers recruited high-achieving Black and White students from Stanford University, most of whom were sophomores, and matched them according to their incoming SAT scores. The Black students and the White students had presumably similar capabilities, based on similar SAT performance.

Then the researchers put these students into an inherently stressful testing situation. They gave them a challenging thirty-minute section from the Graduate Record Examination (GRE) subject test in English literature, typically taken by college seniors applying to graduate school, and told them they were testing verbal ability. When the students' scores were compared, what the researchers found was that, under this high-pressure test-taking circumstance, where all the students were in a way being pushed beyond their current levels of achievement, the White students at Stanford on average outperformed the Black students, even when they were evenly matched for SAT scores coming in. There was a performance gap, but why?

Steele and his colleagues hypothesized that when high-performing, high-achieving Black students who are very invested in doing well in school are put in a high-pressure test-taking situation, where intellectual ability is believed to be relevant to the task, they are likely to experience performance anxiety associated with stereotype threat—anxiety that might suppress the students' performance. To test the hypothesis, the researchers manipulated the experimental design in a variety of ways. In the first example described above, a key condition in the experiment was the fact that they had introduced the test as "diagnostic" of the students' intellectual ability. Under this condition a statistically significant performance gap resulted between Black and White student performance. However, when they gave the test with a different set of instructions—instructions that explicitly stated that the test was not a measure of intellectual ability but simply a laboratory task used to study approaches to problem solving—the difference in Black student performance was dramatic. In the "diagnostic" version of the experiment, Black students performed one full standard deviation below the White students. In the "nondiagnostic" version, Black and White students performed equally well. The racial stereotypes about Black academic performance were made irrelevant by reframing the test and the task in this simple way. Even though the same difficult test questions were used in both versions of the experiment, in the nondiagnostic version, the performance anxiety was reduced and the performance improved.[36]

Steele and other researchers have replicated these results over and over, in a variety of contexts, and found the same effect in other domains. For example, Steele, Steven Spencer, and Diane Quinn demonstrated that stereotype threat lowers the performance of talented female math students on a challenging math test, but when the same test was presented as one on which men and women were expected to perform equally well (thereby reducing the threat of a gendered stereotype about women's performance), the women did indeed perform as well as the men on the difficult test and significantly better than the women in the "stereotype still relevant" test condition.[37]

Steele and his colleagues hypothesized that when equally prepared Black students failed to do as well as their White counterparts in the same room, they were thinking about their racial group membership and the associated stigma, and such thoughts were at the root of the performance anxiety. To test this idea, a new variation was introduced to the experiments. Researchers asked students to complete eighty "fill in the blank" word items just before they were given the challenging test items. Each of the words on the list had two letters missing.

Some of the words had been pre-tested by the researchers and they knew that they could be completed to form "stereotype-relevant" words. For example, a student thinking about racial stereotypes might quickly fill in the missing letters for "_ _ ce" to spell "race" rather than "face" or "rice" or some other choice. Steele and his colleagues found that indeed the Black students wrote stereotype-related words more often than the White students, suggesting that race was on their minds before they took the test. This effect was particularly strong when students had been told that they were about to take a test measuring their intellectual ability. Black students in this diagnostic version listed more stereotype-relevant words than Black students who had received the nondiagnostic instructions prior to taking the test. The instructions did not seem to make a difference for White students, who made few stereotype-related word completions in either case.[38]

How does stereotype threat impede test-taking performance for Black students? In some of the experiments, computers were used to administer the tests, which allowed the researchers to study the test-taking behavior of the students in some detail. Steele writes, "Black students taking the test under stereotype threat seemed to be trying too hard rather than not hard enough. They reread the questions, reread the multiple choices, rechecked their answers, more than when they were not under stereotype threat. The threat made them inefficient on a test that, like most standardized tests, is set up so that thinking long often means thinking wrong, especially on difficult items like the ones we used."[39]

One of the most interesting variations of this series of experiments has fascinating practical implications. In this experimental scenario, researchers asked one group of students to check off a box indicating racial-group membership before they took the test. In another version, every other condition was kept the same, except that the researchers omitted those boxes. Black students who had no box to check were more likely to perform at the same level as White students than those Black students who were asked to indicate their race by checking a box at the beginning. Presumably, the act of asking students to identify their race before the test began was sufficient to trigger the performance anxiety of stereotype threat and suppress the performance of the Black students participating in the experiment.

Of course, checking boxes is currently a routine part of the experience of taking standardized tests like the SAT. The gap in performance between Black and White students on such tests is common knowledge and routinely discussed in the national media. If the box checking suppressed African American student performance in the laboratory among high-achieving Stanford students, is it possible that the same thing happens in real-life test-taking situations? Why not offer the tests without asking for racially identifying information, or if such information is needed for data-collection purposes, wait until after the test is over to collect it—perhaps placing the demographic questions at the end? (I have made this suggestion to a colleague I know at the Educational Testing Service, the publisher of the SAT and similar tests, but I haven't seen any movement in that direction.)

According to the work of Steele and Geoffrey L. Cohen and their associates, stereotype threat is most likely to impact high-achieving students who are highly identified with school. The dilemma may be particularly acute when students feel uncertain about their own ability or belonging. Many students experience this kind of uncertainty during their first year of college, so stigmatized students entering a new academic environment are particularly vulnerable to stereotype threat. Stigmatized students must face the threatening possibility that should their performance be inadequate, their failure will only underscore the racial stereotype of alleged intellectual inferiority.[40]

What does stereotype threat sound like in the real world, outside the experimental laboratory? Listen to these quotes from focus groups with first-year students of color at a predominantly White college, collected as part of a project I designed to assess intellectual engagement in that environment. Said one:

> Sometimes you wonder because you are a woman of color, or a person of color, if someone treats you a certain way, is it because of what your race is or is it something else? You don't know. You have this other factor that other people don't have, and you're wondering did she act that way towards me because I'm Black or did she act this way toward me for another reason?

Another talked about the burden of representing her entire group:

> I have an increased sense of responsibility here not to fail, not to, I don't know, just to represent myself as being a proper young lady, maybe more because I'm in a White atmosphere where most people here haven't met another Black person unless they were on the television, and you have to project, I don't know, just a certain amount of respect for yourself.

The visibility of one's token status adds to the pressure:

> [White students] don't realize that they don't have to think about being White all the time, but in situations, you have to

think about being the only Black one, like in your class, and your professor is going to know that you skipped class [everyone laughs]. They always know YOUR name.

Said another:

I don't know if it's self-imposed, but I always feel like I have to prove that I'm not here because of affirmative action. Like I always feel that I have to speak up in class, that I have to make myself visible to make sure that the professor knows that I am doing my work, that I know what is going on, that I have some creative intelligence. I feel like I constantly have to get the best grade in the class for me to feel better, and just prove myself maybe even to the White students who may be looking at me going, "Oh, she got here because of affirmative action."

The pressure not to prove the stereotype of intellectual inferiority means one cannot reveal weakness, or ask for assistance, even when justified in doing so, as this young woman explained:

I felt a lot of pressure too, never to ask for an extension. I wanted to be this superwoman where I never had a conflict in a schedule or I never got sick, or any of those normal things, and the first time that I did [ask for an extension], I felt really kind of bad about it.

Another added:

I thought I would be confident in my academic work, but I've really struggled with feeling comfortable going to my professors and getting the help that I need.

What is hopeful about our new understanding of stereotype threat and related theories is that they can guide us to
change how we teach and what we say. As Steele puts it: "Although stereotypes held by the larger society may be hard to
change, it is possible to create educational niches in which negative stereotypes are not felt to apply—and which permit a
sense of trust that would otherwise be difficult to sustain."[41]
Receiving honest feedback that you can trust as unbiased is critical to reducing stereotype threat and improving academic performance. How you establish that trust with the possibility of
stereotype swirling around is the question. The key to doing
this seems to be found in clearly communicating both high
standards and assurance of belief in the student's capacity to
reach those standards.

Again the work of Steele and Cohen offers important in-
sights. To investigate how a teacher might gain the trust of a
student when giving feedback across racial lines, they created
a scenario in which Black and White Stanford University students were asked to write essays about a favorite teacher. The
students were told that the essays would be considered for publication in a journal about teaching, and that they would receive
feedback from a reviewer who they were led to believe was
White. A Polaroid snapshot was taken of each student and at-
tached to the essay as it was turned in, signaling to the students
that the reviewer would be able to identify the race of the essay
writer. Several days later the students returned to receive the
reviewer's comments, with the opportunity to "revise and re-
submit" the essay. What was varied in the experiment was how
the feedback was delivered.

When the feedback was given in a constructive but critical
manner, Black students were more suspicious than White students that the feedback was racially biased, and consequently,

the Black students were less likely than the White students to rewrite the essay for further consideration. The same was true when the critical feedback was buffered by an opening statement praising the essay, such as, "There were many good things about your essay." However, when the feedback was introduced by a statement that conveyed a high standard (reminding the writer that the essay had to be of publishable quality) and high expectations (assuring the student of the reviewer's belief that with effort and attention to the feedback, the standard could be met), the Black students not only responded positively by revising the essays and resubmitting them, but they did so at a higher rate than the White students in the study.[42]

The particular combination of the explicit communication of high standards and the demonstrated assurance of the teacher's belief in the student's ability to succeed (as evidenced by the effort to provide detailed, constructive feedback) was a powerful intervention for Black students. Describing this two-pronged approach as "wise criticism," Cohen and Steele demonstrated that it was an exceedingly effective way to generate the trust needed to motivate Black students to make their best effort. Even though the criticism indicated that a major revision of the essay would be required to achieve the publication standard, Black students who received "wise criticism" felt ready to take on the challenge, and did. Indeed, "they were more motivated than any other group of students in the study —as if this combination of high standards and assurance was like water on parched land, a much needed but seldom received balm."[43]

FROM THEORY TO PRACTICE: WHAT CAN WE DO?

What, then, are the practical implications of Steele and his colleagues' research? What are some specific strategies for teachers, mentors, and other adults to consider in an effort to reduce stereotype threat and increase trust in cross-racial interactions?

1. Make standards for evaluation explicit. Establish high standards and make clear to students what the criteria are for meeting them. When standards are made explicit, students are more likely to trust and respond to relevant criticism. Emphasize "effective effort" as the key to success, rather than "innate ability."

2. Avoid overpraising for mediocre work. Students will perceive this as a sign of lowered expectations, and another reason not to trust the feedback.

3. Normalize help-seeking behaviors. For example, if all students are required to meet with the professor early in the semester or after the first exam, any stigma that students of color might feel seeking help outside of class is reduced.

4. When possible, include diversity of perspectives. Racial and cultural inclusivity in the curriculum and the teaching materials will communicate to the student that members of her group are valued and may increase the student's sense of trust.

5. Encourage cross-group interaction in class. Consider assigning working groups rather than allowing students to choose group members themselves. Fostering interaction across racial lines or other lines of difference helps reduce stereotyping among classmates and increases the climate of trust in the classroom. However, clustering students of color within small groups is preferable to "tokenizing" them (placing no more than one student of color per group).

6. Revise your view of intelligence. Indeed, educators can revise their view of intelligence as an innate fixed capacity and can challenge those well-ingrained societal notions of

racial hierarchies of intellectual ability. Students, too, can reevaluate their own assumptions about intelligence—not just other people's intelligence but their own as well.

Many students, like many teachers, believe their intelligence (or lack of it) is a fixed, unchanging characteristic. Years of family members, friends, and teachers remarking, "What a smart boy/girl you are!" certainly reinforces this personal theory of intelligence. The alternate view of intelligence as changeable—as something that can be developed—is less commonly fostered, but can be. The educator Verna Ford has summed up this alternate theory for use with young children quite succinctly: "Think you can—work hard—get smart."[44] Research by the educational psychologist Carol Dweck suggests that those young people who hold a belief in fixed intelligence see academic setbacks as an indicator of limited ability. They are highly invested in appearing smart, and consequently avoid those tasks that might suggest otherwise. Rather than exerting more effort to improve their performance, they are likely to conclude, "I'm not good at that subject" and move on to something else. Students who have the view of intelligence as malleable are more likely to respond to academic setbacks as a sign that more effort is needed, and then exert that effort. They are more likely to face challenges head-on rather than avoid them in an effort to preserve a fixed definition of oneself as "smart."[45] The theory of intelligence as malleable—something that expands as the result of effective effort—fosters an academic resilience that serves its believers well.

The researchers Joshua Aronson, Carrie Fried, and Catherine Good wondered if a personal theory of intelligence as malleable might foster a beneficial academic resilience for students of color vulnerable to stereotype threat. Specifically, they speculated that if Black students believed that their intellectual capacity was not fixed but expandable through their own effort, the negative stereotypes that others hold about their intellectual ability might be less damaging to their academic performance. To introduce this alternative view of intelligence, they designed a study in which Black and White college students were recruited to serve as pen-pal mentors to disadvantaged elementary school students. The task of the college students was to write letters of encouragement to their young mentees, urging them to do their best in school. However, one group of college students was instructed to tell their mentees to think of intelligence as something that was expandable through effort, and in preparation for writing the letters, they were given compelling information, drawn from contemporary research in psychology and neuroscience, about how the brain itself could be modified and expanded by new learning. The real subjects of the study, however, were the college students, not their pen pals. Although the letter writing was done in a single session, the college students exposed to the malleable theory of intelligence seemed to benefit from exposure to the new paradigm. Both Black and White students who learned about the malleability of intelligence improved their grades more than did students who did not receive this information. The benefit was even more striking for Black students, who reported enjoying academics more, saw academics as more important, and had significantly higher grades at the end of the academic quarter than those Black students who had not been exposed to this brief but powerful intervention.[46]

What worked with college students also worked with seventh graders. Lisa Sorich Blackwell, Kali Trzesniewski, and Carol Dweck created an opportunity for some seventh-grade students in New York City to read and discuss a scientific article about how intelligence develops, and its malleability. A comparable group of seventh-grade students did not learn this information, but read about memory and mnemonic strategies instead. Those students who learned about the malleability of intelligence subsequently demonstrated higher academic motivation, better academic behavior, and higher grades in mathematics than those who had learned about memory. Interestingly, girls, who have been shown by Steele and his colleagues to be vulnerable to gender stereotypes about math performance, did equal to or better than boys in math following the "intelligence is malleable" intervention, while girls in the other group performed well below the boys in math. As was the case with the Aronson, Fried, and Good study, the intervention with the seventh graders was quite brief—in this case only three hours—yet the impact was significant.[47] Embracing a theory of intelligence as something that can develop—that can be expanded through effective effort—is something that all of us can do to counteract the legacy of scientific racism, reduce the impact of stereotype threat, and increase the achievement of all of our students.

BREAKING THE SILENCE ABOUT RACE

I have shown how the dynamics of race—in a society in which racist ideology is still deeply embedded, though not always apparent—can affect the achievement of students of color. Cohen and Steele's work on effective feedback, and the other research discussed above, points to the possibility of counteracting the effects of racial stereotypes. But how can we develop these and other strategies if we are not able to talk freely about the continuing effects of racism? How can we overcome the unconscious impact of internalized stereotypes if we are not able to bring them to consciousness through dialogue? This dialogue among adults is important of course not just for the academic performance of students of color, but also for the effective preparation of all of our students who will live in an increasingly multiracial, multiethnic world.

Students look to their teachers for guidance and help for living in an increasingly diverse and complex society, and educators are becoming more aware of the need to prepare their students to live in a multiracial society. Yet this is a world with which the current teaching force has limited experience. Most teachers in the United States are White teachers who were raised and educated in predominantly White communities. Their knowledge of communities of color and their cultures is typically quite limited. One way to address this deficiency in teachers' experiences is to provide them with antiracist, multicultural education courses or programs.

The project that I will describe here briefly attempted to do just that. A two-year demonstration project, funded by the Carnegie Corporation, investigated the combined effect of interventions involving teachers, students, and parents in a small northeastern school district with an increasing school population of color (presently 24 percent).[48] Although the project had three components, an after-school cultural identity group program for middle school students, a series of parent outreach workshops, and a professional development course for educators, it is the professional development initiative that will be the focus of discussion here.

The initiative consisted of a professional development course that required participants (twenty-four teachers/semester) to examine closely their own sense of racial identity and their attitudes toward other groups as well as develop effective antiracist curricula and educational practices that are affirming of student identities and that support positive achievement for all students. It was assumed that teachers must look at their own racial identity in order to be able to support the positive development of their students' racial/ethnic identities. They

71

must also be able to engage in racial dialogue themselves in order to facilitate student conversation.

The professional development course, Effective Anti-Racist Classroom Practices for All Students, was specifically designed to help educators recognize the personal, cultural, and institutional manifestations of racism and to become more proactive in response to racism within their school settings.[49] Topics covered included an examination of the concepts of prejudice, racism, White privilege, and internalized oppression. In addition, theories of racial identity development for both Whites and people of color were discussed, along with an investigation of the historical connection between scientific racism, intelligence testing, and assumptions about the "fixed nature" of student intellectual capacity. The implications of these ideas for classroom practice were explicitly discussed. Course activities included lectures, videos, small and large group discussions, and exercises. Between class meetings, participants wrote short reflection papers in response to the assigned readings, and engaged in topical assignments such as an analysis of cultural stereotypes, omissions, and distortions in their curricular materials. They were also encouraged to actively examine their own expectations and assumptions about the academic potential of students of color. In all, eighty-three educators voluntarily participated in this demonstration project.

Eighty-five percent of the participants were White, and 15 percent were people of color (primarily Latino). Most of the Latino teachers were from a neighboring school district; they were offered slots in the course on a space-available basis. The teaching force of the district in which the project was based was 99.9 percent White. In two of the four semesters that the course was offered, the class was made up entirely of White participants. Sixty-two percent of the participants were elementary school classroom teachers or specialists, 19 percent were working with high school students, and 13 percent were working at the middle school level. Five percent of the participants were district-level administrators. A veteran group of educators, the median number of years of experience was fourteen.

As part of the course requirement, participants were asked to develop an "action plan," as a way of applying what they learned in the course to their own school context. In order to assess the impact of the course on the teachers' role as agents of change, the action plans produced were categorized in terms of their ability to effect change in three areas of schooling: relationships among school and community members, the curriculum, and the institution's efforts regarding support services for students of color.[50] In all, fifty-nine action plans were analyzed.[51] While some plans were just that, plans that had not yet been acted on, most could be considered "works in progress"; the educators had already initiated steps in their proposed action.

Fifty-six percent of the plans involved some effort to make the curriculum more inclusive of people of color. Demonstrating a common beginning step for educators just starting to think about antiracist education, several of the plans involved developing bibliographies and purchasing multicultural books and other classroom materials. While this may seem like a rather inconsequential action, it can have significant impact. For example, one teacher's action plan defined the problem as the "one size fits all" curriculum that was being mandated at the state level. She wrote,

> The problem is the absence of multicultural book titles in themes pertaining to Massachusetts Frameworks. When a unit is studied everyone reads the same book. This is good in the beginning to explain and teach all aspects of the novel; plot, characters, setting. But once students are aware of the parts,

73

they do not all need to read the same novel. It is important that they read novels that reflect their own sex/culture/religion based on their reading ability.

Her plan, already under way, was to "make a list of multicultural novels, with varied reading, and interest levels, for each theme in grade eight English class with Massachusetts Frameworks notation, and persuade the eighth-grade teachers to use them." She had learned in the course about the importance of affirming the identities of her students, so that they could see themselves reflected in the classroom and feel included in the learning process rather than on the margins of it, and she was determined to put that new understanding into action, not just in her own classroom but throughout the school.

Thirty percent of the action plans highlighted antiracist educational practices at the interpersonal level, focusing on relationships between teachers and students or teachers and parents. Given that most of the course participants were classroom teachers, and the course content specifically addressed raising expectations for students of color, it was not surprising that teachers who wanted to effect change often chose to do so by focusing on particular students. Eight of the action plans specifically dealt with communicating high expectations to students of color. A powerful example of one of these plans was provided by a young White teacher who was trying to help a Puerto Rican girl who had already failed her class twice. She wrote:

> I was even hesitant about calling home to her parents. I am ashamed to admit that my first year with [Ana] I made a lot of mistakes. I assumed her lower ability was due to lack of initiative. Maybe she had a terrible home life, which prevented

her from getting things done outside of school. Rather than actually investigating my assumptions I spent the semester taking it easy on her. I thought I was being compassionate and caring, but in reality I was sending a negative message, that not completing her assignments was okay.

When I first started teaching I had a really difficult class with several minorities. I had discipline problems, so I discussed these issues with the principal. He gave me some suggestions, but what most stuck out was when he said, "Check with me before you call some of these kids' parents." For some reason I felt fear or maybe intimidation from that statement. ... This semester I called home, I have never called home before. That made a big difference. She has a wonderful family, a hard-working family. Her parents are very concerned.... All of these false assumptions were based on the internalized stereotypical generalizations regarding people of color, which in fact clouded my judgment and ultimately undermined how I taught [Ana]. At the time I thought I was doing a good job, but now I realize she had been short-changed. This semester I am on her like glue to do her work.

Her student's performance changed dramatically—from failing grades to an A- average. In addition, her developing relationship with this Latina student helped her see more clearly the way racism was operating in the school, and she began to raise these issues in her class. She wrote in her closing reflection paper:

I have also made an effort to bring up social inequities in the school by setting aside time during class to discuss these issues. I give each student air time to voice his/her opinion. Although not math related sometimes the racial comments regarding experiences in school warrant these discussions. Students need to know that these issues are real and apparent within our school and in our community. Some know all too well from firsthand experience.

Although this young teacher was brave enough to raise these issues in her math class, taking action beyond the classroom was much less common for other educators who participated in the class. Perhaps actions that challenge institutional policies and practices were less frequent than the other types because such interventions seemed beyond the average teacher's sphere of influence and felt too risky. Despite the risks, however, two Latino teachers decided to do a comparative analysis of disciplinary actions taken against White and Latino students in their school. Their project was viewed with considerable suspicion by their principal, and in fact their results revealed a pattern of Puerto Rican students receiving longer punishments than other students. The teachers shared their findings with other Hispanic teachers in the school, but did not confront the principal. Instead they decided among themselves to develop alternate strategies for dealing with discipline problems.

> We organized a meeting with the Hispanic teachers and it was a very successful one. We presented the project concerning student discipline and we came up with the idea to have the student come after school to meet with the teacher before sending them to the office.

In another school, a White teacher shared her new sense of empowerment with her students to bring about institutional change.

As I thought about racism in our society, I began to think about what I could do in my classroom. How can I help to change things? And it seemed to me that all of my students needed to feel empowered. One of the things that happened was that kids couldn't stay for after-school activities because there was no after-school bus. So a class took on the project of lobbying for a bus. They did a survey in the school and they spoke to the school council to present their findings. The final result was that we have a bus now for two days a week. Their study has also been used to apply for a grant for next year. This class experienced a real sense of empowerment. I hope this experience will encourage them to work constructively for change.... Recently two students said to me, "I don't understand why we don't have a Puerto Rican festival here at [school]. I said, "Well do you want one?" And they said, "Yeah, well, of course we want one." So I said I would help it happen. Since then, two girls started and planned a festival. It's become a real lesson in empowerment.

While the level of commitment and degree of initiative varied greatly across the action plans, it seemed clear that most of the educators emerged from the course with a heightened sense of both their responsibility and their power to address issues of inequity in the school, to become allies to the students of color in their school, and to be antiracist role models for all students. Such awareness can only be a step in the right direction for improving student performance. Perhaps the significance of the learning is best captured in the closing quote of this educator, a woman with thirty years of experience in public education.

As I write this action plan, I have to ask myself why I did not see the need for this or other services for children of color before taking this course. The only answer that I can think of is that I was insensitive to those needs and blind to the effects of racism that were all around me. The White privilege audit that we did and the school/classroom audit helped to bring those issues into focus for me. More than any course I have ever taken, this one has helped to open my eyes and shock me into taking some positive concrete steps toward combating racist attitudes in my daily life. I intend to continue the process of becoming more sensitive to the needs of students of color. I sincerely hope that we, as a school system, can capitalize on the momentum and energy generated by this course and build a truly multicultural environment for our students.

Did this demonstration project improve student performance district-wide, enough to close the achievement gap? I can't say that it did, because the project did not continue beyond the two years of funding, not long enough to see systemic change. We do know that *individual* students improved their performance in response to *individual* teachers' antiracist efforts.

I believe that this kind of antiracist professional development is extremely important in transforming practice, and that there should be more of it. Should it be mandatory? I am often asked this question. My response is based in my experience. The most effective work that I've done has been with educators who were participating voluntarily. And yet when we talk about voluntary audiences, people often say, "Well, you are just preaching to the choir." My response to that is always that the choir needs rehearsal!

It is hard to do this work, and gathering with others who are like-minded or who are focused on the same thing can in fact lead you to feel more empowered to do it. The educators who participated in the Massachusetts study went back to their classrooms, talked to their colleagues, and tried new strategies that they hadn't tried before. They had gathered with other, similarly motivated folks with the result that—to continue with the choir analogy—they were learning to sing better. And when you sing well, you encourage other people to sing with you. I have always thought about this professional development work in this way: as gathering those who are interested and helping them to think about how to expand their own spheres of influence to bring about change through the ripple effect. Those educators who might never volunteer for such a course are inevitably influenced by the momentum generated by those working around them. And some of them learn by example that they might like to sing, too.

BEYOND INDIVIDUAL ACTION TO SYSTEMIC CHANGE

Singing in concert with others leads to a more powerful result than singing alone, and of course, change happens more quickly at the institutional level when the focus shifts from the individual to the systemic—to the policies and practices that cut across classrooms. In their recent book, *Courageous Conversations about Race,* Glenn Singleton and Curtis Linton make the important point that "we must not mistake personal anti-racist leadership for Systemic Equity Anti-Racism Transformation. Individuals and schools must be part of an entire community of courageous, passionate and mutually supportive leaders in the district."[52] In order for system-wide change to take place, there must be leadership at the highest levels to support the examination of continuing educational inequities, especially when there is community resistance to doing so.

Singleton and Linton offer as a case example the Lemon Grove School District near San Diego, California, a district that has been engaged in a system-wide antiracist focus for five years. In 2001 Lemon Grove was one of the most diverse school districts in San Diego County, with 34 percent of its students Latino, 34 percent White, 22 percent African American, and 10 percent representing other groups of color. Like many districts, there was an achievement gap that fell along racial lines, and a history of racial tension. Disproportionate numbers of Latino and African American students scored in the lowest quartiles, and only a few were in the top quartile. In an effort to bring about change and close the achievement gap, in 2001 the superintendent, Dr. McLean King, released a vision statement emphasizing a system-wide focus on equity.[53] Like many districts, he identified the school mission as one of engaging and supporting "all students in achieving high academic standards." In his vision he advocated for "a culture that embraces diversity, respects all cultures, and ensures the development and implementation of educational programs that maximize academic achievement for all students regardless of race, color, or creed." While all of this was positive, it was not unusual. What set Dr. King's vision statement apart from others I have seen was his explicit mention of the role of race and the personal responsibility that all of the educators in his district had to engage in self-reflection. He said, "It is equally important that all school leaders are personally aware of the role race plays in perpetuating a system of bias, prejudice, and inequity. Such awareness and each individual's personal commitment are critical to the creation of a school environment that is free from racism." He concluded his vision statement with these words:

> I charge the entire staff and educational community of the Lemon Grove School District to take risks by closely examining the role we each play in changing a system that has allowed this unacceptable achievement gap to emerge within this district. All educators in Lemon Grove will make a personal

commitment and be held professionally accountable for the achievement of this vision.

We have the capacity; however, we must have the will to make a difference![54]

With that kind of clear and powerful leadership, it is not surprising that Lemon Grove is making significant progress toward its goal of closing the achievement gap. Historically a low-performing school district, in the five years that this effort has been under way, the district has consistently scored better than schools with similar demographics. Despite the fact that 65 percent of the students are economically disadvantaged (eligible for free or reduced lunch), 20 percent have limited English skills, and state funding per pupil is slightly below the state average, the district is making impressive gains. In 2004 Black students in five of the eight schools and Latino students in four of the eight schools improved at a rate greater than their White counterparts, suggesting that the racial achievement gap is closing rapidly. At the same time, all students are showing achievement gains. Singleton and Linton conclude, "The transformation occurring in the district follows our equity definition: Raise the achievement of all students while narrowing the gaps between the highest and lowest performing students; and eliminating the racial predictability and disproportionality of which student groups occupy the highest and lowest achievement categories."[55]

The case of Lemon Grove clearly illustrates that a commitment to breaking the silence about race at all levels of the educational system can indeed lead to improving performance for all students. We know what to do. We just have to have the courage and commitment to do it.

THREE

"What Kind of Friendship Is That?"

The Search for Authenticity, Mutuality, and Social Transformation in Cross-Racial Relationships

In her recent book, *Some of My Best Friends: Writings on Inter-racial Friendships,*[1] editor Emily Bernard invited a multiracial group of writers to join her in reflecting on the possibility of friendship across color lines. Women and men of diverse backgrounds attempted to address Bernard's key questions: Which ingredients make interracial friendships possible? Which factors destroy them? Could individual friendships be the answer to some of our larger social problems? I was particularly struck by one writer's answer to Bernard's questions. In his provocative essay, "Secret Colors," David Mura, a Japanese American man, wrote:

> Yes interracial friendships with whites are possible. Certainly they are possible if the person of color thinks of himself as white or desires to be thought of as white—that is, if the person of color forces from his consciousness the differences in his experience of race or how he might view himself differently

from his white friend. Such friendships are also possible if race is never discussed as part of the relationship (some interracial marriages even function in this way). In such instances, the person of color might be aware of differences and difficulties due to racial issues, but remains silent about them. Instead, the person of color suppresses his true feelings and presents a version of himself he thinks will please, or at least not trouble, his white friend.

Under such conditions, friendship is possible: but we might ask then: What kind of friendship is that?[2]

What kind of friendship is that? Indeed, Mura's question highlights the core dimension of those relationships that go beyond the superficiality of warm acquaintanceship or the politeness of congenial collegiality. Genuine friendship generates enough trust to allow for honest exchange between oneself and the other about matters large and small, and permits the sharing of one's true thoughts and feelings, even when those thoughts and feelings are troubling to the receiver. Genuine friendship is characterized by authenticity and mutuality, which is life giving and soul satisfying. Genuine friendship, repeating the words of the psychologist Jean Baker Miller as presented in Chapter 1, leaves us feeling "seen, heard, and understood."[3]

Perhaps such friendship is rare under the best of circumstances. Can it exist between those who have learned from firsthand experience or secondhand history to be wary of one another? Can it exist between those who have breathed in the smog of cultural assumptions of individual and cultural racial and ethnic superiority and those who have been labeled as inferior by the dominant culture? Can we have the kind of relationships across lines of race and ethnicity that are truly authentic and mutual? And in the end, what difference does it make?

In her classic 1988 essay, "Connections, Disconnections, and Violations," Miller wrote eloquently about the constructive power of relational connections and the potentially destructive force of relational disconnections and violations. What happens when our experience *is validated* by another person in a mutually empathic relationship? We feel a strong sense of connection. We experience what Dr. Miller calls the "five good things." When a relationship is mutually reinforcing, it gives you a feeling of increased zest, a sense of empowerment, greater self-knowledge, increased self-worth, and most importantly in the context of a friendship, a desire for more connection.[4] Those five good things are indeed a powerful incentive to seek mutual engagement with friends and loved ones. Certainly genuine friendships are rooted in love, but love is not enough.

In her reflection on interracial friendship, Emily Bernard observed, "In my experience being loved isn't the same thing as being seen."[5] Building on this theme, David Mura describes the ways he was invisible to his White friends and to himself in the context of their relationships.

> For many years, I lived an unconscious life that constantly tried to repress anything in my experience that related to race; the friends I had then were comfortable with that repression. When I started to break down that repression, I had to look not only at my identity, but at their identity, at the ways they were comfortable with that repression and what that told me about the way they saw me, about what they meant when they said they loved me. (After all, Scarlett loved Mammy, and where did that get Mammy?)[6]

Love does not guarantee equality, reciprocity, authenticity, or mutuality. But the variety of love one finds in friendship demands it. Can White people and people of color move beyond the inherited inequality embedded in our shared history—the history of Scarlett O'Hara and her enslaved Black servant Mammy being just one example—to forge the kind of authentic relational connections that Miller describes? For me, the answer to this question is yes, it *is* possible. I say yes because I have such friendships, but I recognize that they are not easily forged, and our capacity to form them is shaped by our own developmental process and willingness to engage with the historical and contemporary meaning of race in our society.

WHAT'S IDENTITY GOT TO DO WITH IT?

In childhood, who becomes a friend is governed largely by convenience and proximity; but in adolescence, and certainly in adulthood, we make more active choices. Our choice of friends is shaped in part, if not wholly, by our sense of self-definition, particularly in adolescence and adulthood. But self-definition does not emerge in a vacuum. It is shaped by a lifetime of social interactions, molded by messages received about who we are in the world, how others perceive us, and with whom we should seek connection. In a society where racial group membership is still a meaningful social characteristic, the development of racial identity is relevant to how our social connections are formed and maintained. I have written extensively about the meaning, significance, and development of racial identity for both Whites and people of color.[7] Here I want to briefly summarize the developmental process that unfolds in the context of a race-conscious society.

Let me begin with the assumption that in a society where racial group membership is emphasized, the development of a racial identity will occur in some form in everyone. Given the dominant/subordinate relationship of Whites and people of color in this society, however, it is not surprising that this developmental process unfolds differently for each. But regardless of one's racial/ethnic background, I hold that a positive sense of oneself as a member of one's group (which is not based on any assumed superiority) is important for emotional well-being.[8] For the purpose of illustration, I want to talk about this from the perspective of people of color, drawing upon the work of the psychologist William Cross.[9]

In childhood, the young person is likely to have absorbed many of the beliefs and values of the dominant White culture —regardless of his or her own cultural background. The pervasive influence of the media, the socializing impact of school, can override countervailing messages at home, to the extent that those are also present. If there is the opportunity of proximity, it is common for children of color who live in racially mixed neighborhoods to have White friends at this stage of development. Of course, given the considerable social segregation, many young people grow up in neighborhoods where they don't have opportunity or proximity with respect to children of different races. But where there is such proximity, certainly it is common for young children to have racially mixed groups of friends. Typically the personal salience of race is minimized for young children of color.

But in adolescence that starts to change. New experiences may bring new awareness of the meaning of one's racial group membership. For example, when I interviewed young Black women who had grown up in predominantly White communities, one young woman described an interaction she had with a White girlfriend in junior high school. She said that when her friend introduced her to another White classmate, the classmate gave the Black girl's friend "a look like, 'I can't believe you have a Black friend.'" The Black girl vividly recalled her friend saying, "She's not really Black, she just went to Florida and got a really dark tan." "And that upset me incredibly," she recounted, "because it was like, What? Yes I am, wait a second here."

There are other examples that are perhaps not quite so obvious. Issues related to race come up in ways that we don't always anticipate. My children grew up in western Massachusetts, in the city of Northampton, where we lived for many years prior to my move to Atlanta to become the president of Spelman. When my oldest son was in elementary school, he invited a White child home for an afternoon visit. It was the first time this child had been to our house, but they were friends from school. They were playing a computer game in the basement, seated at the computer, and my husband was within earshot. And he heard the young friend, the visitor, say to my son, "My brother says Black people are stupid." Our son did not respond to this out-of-the-blue remark. They just kept playing the game; he ignored it. My husband, however, heard the conversation, came up the stairs, and said to me, "Who is that kid and what is he doing in our house?" Although our son had ignored the remark, as parents we had to decide whether we would. (We chose not to ignore it, and shared the incident with the young boy's father in a parent-to-parent conversation.)[10] When you least expect it, the issue of race can emerge, even in a context of friendship.

These dynamics are not limited to the domain of race. Class differences, and the assumptions that accompany them, can also create relational complexities. I remember a friendship that I developed in college with a young African American woman. We had very different class backgrounds. She had grown up in the South Bronx. Although she had attended an elite, predominantly White boarding school in high school through a scholarship program, she came from a low-income neighborhood where all of the families were poor, including hers. I grew up in a middle-class family. My father was a college professor and my mother was a public school teacher. And my view of the world was very much shaped by that class experience, that middle-class experience.

I remember having a conversation with this friend, who told me that when we first met, she had been suspicious of me because I smiled too much. In her view, I was a little too happy. And part of that happiness was the fact that I hadn't had to struggle in the ways that she'd had to struggle. I also think of a conversation with a fellow student in graduate school, a Black man I did not know well. We were waiting for a bus, and he asked me what I was going to be doing when I finished graduate school. I told him that maybe I would teach, maybe I'd be a psychotherapist. I wasn't exactly sure. I added, "You know, I just know I don't ever want to be bored." And he looked at me and said, "What is your class background?" "What do you mean?" I replied. And he said, "Well, where did you get the idea that work was supposed to be entertaining?" The notion that work should be fulfilling and not just something you do because you have to support yourself or your family or to make ends meet clearly came out of my class background. Class, like race, influences how we view the world, and ultimately influences how we interact with other people.

Sometimes the situations among friends, or potential friends, may be more subtle—communicating that one's racial status is not to be acknowledged or addressed. One of the writers in Emily Bernard's book is Trey Ellis, an African American writer who describes himself as a "cultural mulatto."[11] He means by that that he grew up in White neighborhoods and experienced himself as between cultures in many ways. Interestingly, he found that it was more comfortable in some respects to be friends with Jewish classmates, because they were also somewhat on the margin of the mainstream White culture in his school community. In writing about his close adolescent friendship with two Jewish boys in his town, Ellis says this:

> I never shared my blackness with them. We never discussed race except dismissively: I don't think of you as black, you're just Trey. Or, I'm not even really Jewish, I'm just a person. For us, somehow, talking about our difference felt tacky. We deftly avoided the subject, the way cultured grownups avoid talking about how much money they make. I didn't tell them that I felt so nervous that I was almost sick whenever a Toys 'R' Us assistant manager followed me around the store, and that I wouldn't breathe right again until I was back out on the street. I didn't tell them that I had been reading *Soul on Ice* or the *Autobiography of Malcolm X,* or listening to Richard Pryor albums every day after school. My blackness was my secret world.[12]

An important aspect of who Trey was remained hidden from his friends, seemingly because he didn't know how to talk to them about it. As in the case of David Mura, an important part of who he was remained invisible to them.

Did these young men have to hide to remain in relationship with their White friends? When they began to actively explore their identity, could their White friends share in that process with them? More often than not the answer to that question is no. To focus on my identity as a person of color inevitably means that it will require my White friend to think about his or her own Whiteness, an act of self-examination that may be uncomfortable to undertake.

It is not uncommon to see White youth and youth of color who have grown up together going their separate ways in adolescence. I think that often it is for exactly this reason: the difficulty in engaging in a conversation about the increased awareness of or experience of encounters with race or racism that the young person of color is beginning to have, on the one hand; and the lack of exploration of their own racial identity that is typical for White youth at that time.

Black teenagers and other youth of color typically begin to explore their racial identity during adolescence, but White youth may wait a long time before they think about what it means to be White. Sometimes they never do. Whether such reflection begins at all is certainly a function of social circumstance and context, and if the context doesn't require it, it may never occur. (I will say more about the implications of this for schools at the end of this chapter.)

David Mura describes the ending of a friendship he had with a White woman in this way:

> I can still recall vividly that walk with Cathy, her querulous tone, her confusion about why I had already broken off a friendship with another mutual white friend. She kept wanting to believe it was just differences in personalities.... She wanted to believe that we did not really view things that differently, that we were on the same side. Yet even as she spoke, she seemed more and more distant from me. I felt she had been talking to herself or to someone else other than me, some vision of me she still clung to. Part of me sensed she'd reached a line and was not going to cross it. I had crossed, and there was no going back for me. She did not want to move, and she could not quite admit that. And yet in another sense, a gulf was revealed that had always been there. Only I hadn't wanted to admit its existence. In a sense, I felt as if I had become a stranger, perhaps even to myself. The new part of me, or the long-buried part of me I'd claimed, remained beyond her view. Because if she truly saw it, she would have to change.[13]

91

CONFLICT AND CONNECTION: A CASE STUDY

The story of cross-racial friendship does not always begin or end in the way that David Mura described. My own story of my friendship with Andrea Ayvazian has been told publicly. We often tell it together.[14] Andrea is a White woman of Armenian ancestry who has worked on issues of social justice for a long time. Today, I count her as one of my closest friends. We met in the context of work, just as young people often meet in school. We have known each other for almost twenty years.

We first met as social justice educators. We were both affiliated with an organization that provided "unlearning racism" workshops. We were paired as a biracial team charged with facilitating a multiday workshop at an institution in the Boston area. We both lived in western Massachusetts, and we had to drive two hours together to get to Boston. We would lead the workshop and then drive back. It had been, as we would say, a particularly tough group. And we spent a lot of time over several sessions talking about what we thought had gone well and what had gone wrong, or what we might do differently. We had to strategize together about how we were going to make it better the next time. It was a challenging workshop to do.

Several things are important about this story of how we got to know each other. One is that we met in the context of work. Particularly in adult relationships, that is often how people come together, people working in a shared environment. We still tend to be socially segregated by geography and real estate. Northampton is not a particularly segregated town—the Black population is small and dispersed throughout the community —but Andrea and I did not live in the same neighborhood. We both have children, but our children did not go to the same school. She and I have similar educational backgrounds, but we didn't go to any of the same colleges or universities. Nothing in particular would have brought us together naturally, except for the context of work. So the workplace is certainly an important place for friendship development, as is the world of higher education, bringing people together whose paths might not otherwise cross.

But another aspect that is important about our relationship is that we began talking about race from the very beginning. In some of the relationships that I have described, race was in the room, but not a subject for discussion. In our case, because of the work we were doing, we had to talk about race from the very beginning. We talked about our own personal experiences with race. We talked to each other and publicly about dealing with challenging racial issues, because that was part of the workshop process. Race was on the table from the very beginning, and I am sure that fact contributed to our ability to connect. We were able to size each other up racially, so to speak, in a very open and overt way.

Yet another factor in this long-term friendship is that when we became friends, we came together not as teacher and learner. Your teacher can be your friend, but on different terms from the kind of relationship that I am describing here. The kind of friendship that gives you those five good things Miller wrote about is really based on mutuality, not on power differential.

Finally, the fact that we were able to come together as equals rather than as teacher and learner in the context of a cross-racial relationship largely had to do with the fact that Andrea had worked on her Whiteness. *I mean something particular about that:* Andrea had thought about what it means to be White in a race-conscious society. She had spent a lot of time prior to our meeting examining her own Whiteness, thinking about what it meant to have privilege, about what it meant to be in a relationship with those who might not have the same

93

privileges. I did not feel, as a person of color, that I needed to teach her what you might call the first things about race. We both had things to learn in our friendship, and over the years we have taught each other many lessons, but we had both done internal work on understanding our racial identities, and the lessons learned were, I would say, in balance.

Bill Ayers, a distinguished professor of education at the University of Illinois at Chicago, articulately describes a different dynamic in a friendship with an older Black activist he knew in the 1960s, much earlier in his life. Looking back on the relationship, he writes:

> Were we friends? We were thrust together by our work, our intimacy almost entirely circumstantial, the stuff of shared risk and common experience. We sang together at community gatherings and prayed together at rallies. We picketed and demonstrated and inevitably, I suppose, found ourselves talking about our hopes and our fears, embraced by the quiet and the dark of night. Yes, I thought at the time, we were friends.
>
> ... Were we friends? I ask myself, and more than 35 years later, the question startles me. There was a shared purpose in our relationship, to be sure—we were building a movement to change the world. We were earnest, driven, flying on a freedom high fueled by action and hope and then more action. I would have said at the time that, yes, we were friends, but now I'm not so sure.
>
> Alex criticized me freely and often, instructed me and corrected me. It never would have occurred to me to answer in kind. I was young, for one thing, and I was stretching. I can think of a dozen practical gifts and lessons Alex bestowed on me ... but I can't think of a thing I gave to him. Were we friends? If friendship asks reciprocity, if a friend finds a way

to be loyal but critical, supportive but demanding, then Alex *was* my friend, and perhaps I failed the core requirements of friendship in return.[15]

Reciprocity is important, but there is something else that is also required, and that is the ability to navigate conflict. In friendships, conflict is inevitable, and even when we don't intend for it to be so, those conflicts often have racial meaning. We have to be willing to name that meaning when we see it. When we don't, disconnection is often the result.

Emily Bernard gives an example of the cost of racial silence in a friendship. Describing what happened between her and Susan, a White friend whom she loved, Bernard writes:

Susan asked me what "the black community" really thought about names like Sheniqua and Tyronda, because "the white community" thought they were just bizarre. As she asked me this question, I watched myself turn, in Susan's eyes, from Emily into "the black community." And I watched her transform herself from Susan who forgot, for a moment, that we had spent hours talking on the phone about our uncanny similarities, down to the cadence of our speech. Completely alike, we said. Completely understood, I felt. It was just a moment, but it changed everything. By the time I got up the nerve to bring it up, it was too late, mostly because I waited for two years, trying to forget it."[16]

Not being able to talk about the significance of race when you see it leads to disconnection.

About two years into our friendship, I had an argument with Andrea. She and I have talked about it together publicly, so I will not be breaking her confidence when I describe that conflict here. What I learned from that argument was the importance of being able to put the issues on the table.

In 1991 we were jointly leading a workshop in St. Louis with a group of clergy. The workshop was focused on unlearning racism and the role of clergy in leading their congregations to greater racial awareness. The participants represented a group of clergy that was both multiracial and multidenominational. The primary focus was on race and racism, but in the course of the workshop, we began to talk about the connections among "isms"—various forms of institutionalized prejudice and discrimination—as we often did: classism, sexism, anti-Semitism, and so forth. In the course of that conversation, controversy emerged among the clergy as to whether heterosexism should be included on the list. There was a wide range of points of view among the clergy in that room about homophobia and homosexuality, as there is among clergy nationwide, and there was open disagreement among them.

Afterward, Andrea and I had a long discussion about the conversation and the varying points of view expressed. I was particularly interested in the opinion of an African American Presbyterian minister in the group, as I had just joined a Presbyterian church—the Martin Luther King Jr. Community Presbyterian Church in Springfield, Massachusetts.

My husband and I were living in Northampton, Massachusetts, a predominantly White community, and we had decided that we wanted to have our children be part of a Black environment, at least some of the time. And so we had sought out a predominantly Black congregation to join, and we found one that we liked in Springfield, a city about thirty minutes away from our home. I was very excited about having just joined. The spirit of the pastor and the congregation had been the primary factors in our choice, not the specifics of the denomination. Although I eventually became aware that there was controversy within the Presbyterian denomination about whether openly gay men and lesbian women could be ordained, this denominational policy was not an issue on which I had focused in choosing that church.

Andrea, however, had been very active in the struggle for civil rights for gay, lesbian, and bisexual people for some time. It was a part of her daily life in many ways. A heterosexual woman living in partnership with a man, she had chosen not to be married to stand in solidarity with her sister, who is a lesbian and who at the time could not legally marry her partner. Andrea had been quite public about this decision, and had even written an article about why she had chosen not to be married.

She was making a clear, active, and involved witness, and I was aware of that. But it was not something that she and I had talked much about until this workshop. In the course of our conversation about the workshop on the plane back from St. Louis, Andrea confronted me about my own heterosexism in a particular way. She said she couldn't believe that I was a member of my new church. How could I, with my politics, be a member of a denomination that was exclusionary? she asked rhetorically. Andrea, who is now the ordained pastor of a United Church of Christ congregation, was at the time a practicing Quaker, and she belonged to a Quaker congregation, which was explicitly open and affirming of everyone, regardless of sexual orientation. Clearly she wanted me to hold my new denomination to the same standard.

I was taken aback by her comment. She knew I had just joined this church, and that I was very excited about it. In response to her question, I said *Hmm* to myself and retreated into the book I was reading on the plane. I didn't engage with her at the time. But Andrea's comment continued to stick in my head, and I was irritated by it, even after we had returned home. It took me a while to put my finger on what was bothering me about it. In the end, what I concluded was that there was a lot of White privilege in her statement and her tone. It was easy for her to say, "You should just join another church." Well, there aren't that many Black churches in western Massachusetts. Trying to find one as open and affirming as the Quakers on this issue probably would have been impossible. And while it had been my message to my children that we should be inclusive and embracing of all people, at the same time I wanted my children to have the uniquely Black religious and community experience that we had found at my new church.

It irked me that she was being so judgmental when she, as a White person of faith, was in a very different circumstance. As a White person willing to change her denomination, she had many predominantly White churches to choose from, with a wider range of political stances on gay rights and ordination. I didn't disagree with her on the substance of the politics; but the Quaker alternative was not going to provide my children with the particular religious and cultural experience that I wanted them to have.

We hadn't been friends that long, a couple of years. And so, at the time, it was a difficult question: Do I want to tell Andrea how irritated I am about this comment, or do I just let it go? I believe that if I had not said anything about it at the time, the outcome would have been similar to Emily Bernard's example —we would not be friends today. We probably would have continued to be collegial, certainly; we worked together. But as friends we probably would have drifted apart, because I would have said to myself, *She doesn't get it.*

Instead of being silent, I called her up and said, "I have to talk to you about something." She asked, "What?" And I said, "I have to tell you, you said something to me on the plane that's been bothering me ever since." She said, "Okay," and I could hear her breathing deeply on the other end of the phone, open but bracing herself in a way. And I proceeded to tell what I thought about her comment.

She listened quietly, and then she said, "You're right." And that made all the difference to me. She acknowledged my point of view and I felt my experience had been validated. We went on to talk about what it meant for her to be at her church; I talked about my ambivalence about being at mine, and why it still felt important to stay. Although we were not in complete agreement, our frank conversation allowed us to continue to deepen our relationship in ways that were very life affirming. The key here is that I challenged her racial privilege, and she was willing to listen. Our friendship moved forward. Had my concern been allowed to fester, perhaps it would have died a premature death, or remained at a more superficial level.

This story would not be complete if I did not also add that she continued to challenge my heterosexual privilege, albeit in a less judgmental way, and I also listened. And when a change in pastoral leadership at the Springfield church resulted in a series of explicitly homophobic sermons, we made the difficult decision to take our children elsewhere and joined a multiracial United Church of Christ congregation that was welcoming to all.

The argument that Andrea and I had in 1991 was our first but not the only conflict in our long friendship. The key to the longevity of our friendship has been the willingness to put our issues on the table. And that is hard to do across racial lines.

SOCIAL CHANGE REQUIRES SOCIAL CONNECTION

Cross-racial communication can be difficult. Why bother? What is the benefit—can't I get the five good things of friendship from someone who looks like me? Anyone who has experienced the phenomenon known as the Spelman sisterhood

—the community of women at Spelman College—knows the answer to that question is yes. The opportunity for mutual relationships with someone who shares your life experience is irreplaceable. But relationships across lines of difference are essential for the possibility of social transformation. Change is needed. None of us can make that change alone. Genuine friendship leads to caring concern. Caring concern leads to action. And we need to take our action from the position of strength that comes from self-knowledge and social awareness. Cross-racial friendships can be a source of both.

Andrea Ayvazian shared these words at the end of an essay we wrote together on the topic of our friendship:

> In the end, I believe the issue is not how I respond to Beverly's Blackness. It is how I have come to understand my own Whiteness. In the end, I believe the issue for me is how I have come to understand social, political, and economic power and my unearned advantage and privilege as a White woman in a racist society. I believe the strongest thing that I bring to our friendship, our relationship, and our connection is an understanding of my Whiteness, something that for several decades, I was helped to not see or to not recognize its significance. It is my understanding of my own Whiteness, not my response to her Blackness, that allows me to interact with Beverly in a way that continues to foster mutuality, connection, and trust.[17]

While the dynamics of friendship are unique in many ways, and uniquely intimate, I believe we can learn some lessons as a society—and as educators—from the examples I have offered here. One lesson is that *human connection requires familiarity and contact.* Gloria Ladson-Billings's *The Dream Keepers: Successful Teachers of African-American Children* is a study of educators who were teaching mostly Black children in urban schools with predominantly Black populations.[18] Some of the teachers who were successful were Black teachers. Some of the teachers who were successful were White teachers. But one of the characteristics of all of these effective teachers was that they made an effort to know the community. They spent time in it. They were not necessarily from the community in which they were teaching or familiar with it when they first got there, but they went out of their way to make home visits, attend church events when children were in the church play, and so on. They did things to connect with the child's out-of-classroom experience.

A second lesson is that *White people and people of color often come to the challenges of cross-racial connection with very different perspectives.* For example, in college, White students and students of color often have a desire to connect with one another across racial lines. But they do so with different expectations. In a study of University of California students, the sociologist Troy Duster observed that White students were interested in interacting with Black students, but they preferred social opportunities such as getting together on a Saturday afternoon and sharing pizza—an informal, unstructured social setting. Black students too shared the desire to connect across racial lines, but they wanted structure around that desire. They preferred to engage with White students in formal settings like classrooms or workshops where issues related to race could be discussed. Typically, White students did not want to participate in those workshops; they didn't necessarily want to talk about power and privilege. They just wanted to be friends—not realizing the ways that unexamined power and privilege could impede the development of such friendships.[19]

Duster's finding resonates with my own experience working on predominantly White campuses. Students of color I have known in my years of teaching often expressed disappointment when few White students chose to come to the educational forums they organized or the diversity workshops that took place. As in Duster's study, they observed that many White students did not want to talk about racial issues in such contexts. They did seem to prefer the social comfort of the familiar—whether the pizza parlor or the campus center. But students of color, particularly African American students, have told me that it is often in such relaxed social environments (with or without alcohol) that unexamined stereotypes emerge in casual language, causing discomfort and the kind of invisibility that Trey Ellis described—discomfort that hangs awkwardly in the air but goes unnamed and undiscussed.

And yet an important lesson of my own experience of cross-racial friendship is that *connection depends on frankness, and a willingness to talk openly about issues of race.* And that may take structures that institutions can help foster. In a society where residential segregation persists and school segregation is increasing, familiarity and contact across racial lines requires intentionality. We need to think about how we can structure meaningful dialogue opportunities.

In Chapter 4 I focus on examples of such opportunities in the context of higher education. Here I will offer community-based examples. For instance, in Atlanta, where I now live, the civic organization Leadership Atlanta each year brings together an intentionally diverse group of seventy community leaders to spend a year meeting in seminars and small discussion groups learning about important social issues in the city (e.g., education, health care, homelessness). The yearlong experience begins, however, with a two-day workshop on race, designed to provide a lens through which all the other seminars will be considered. The focus is on stimulating cross-racial dialogue that has the potential of evolving into cross-racial connections deep enough to support community transformation.

Another helpful example can be found in the work of the Study Circles Resource Center, a national, nonpartisan, nonprofit organization that helps communities bring people together across divides of race, income, age, and political viewpoints to solve community problems, with particular attention to the racial and ethnic dimensions of the problems they address. Although Study Circles staff members are available to offer advice and training, their most powerful resources take the form of their written guides (available in English and Spanish) that motivated citizens can use on their own to guide constructive cross-racial dialogue. The first such text was published in 1992—a guide on racism and race relations designed to provide tools for structured conversations about race that would allow people to deepen their understanding of one another's perspectives across racial lines, and ultimately help them move from dialogue to action and change. Since then it has been used by thousands of study circles across the United States in communities as different from one another as Los Angeles, California, and Lima, Ohio. In 2006 the Study Circles Resource Center published its latest guide, *Facing Racism in a Diverse Nation,* and it is a powerful tool to help communities build the kind of diverse, meaningful dialogue our country needs. The model it offers explicitly guides participants past their fear and anger to take the risks that cross-racial dialogue requires, with the clear goal of moving beyond mere talk to effective action and social change.[20]

As educators we need to find our way into such conversations, not only because they benefit our communities but because they strengthen our capacity to help our students have them. We, whether White or of color, need to deepen our own understanding of the systemic nature of racism, its impact on each of us, and how to interrupt it. Such a shared understanding not only creates common ground for the cultivation of friendship, it also is a prerequisite for the transformative education we need for a more just society.

FOUR

In Search of Wisdom

Higher Education for a
Changing Democracy

Where is the wisdom
we have lost in knowledge?
Where is the knowledge
we have lost in information?

These lines from T. S. Eliot's poem "Choruses from 'The Rock'" were written more than seventy years ago, yet they still resonate with power today.[1] Our students have grown up in the information age. They have easy access to so much information —but will they use it wisely? There are difficult decisions to make in our increasingly complex world. How do we adequately prepare our students for wise ethical and responsible leadership?

This is an important question, because while there are certainly wise students among us, their development may have occurred in spite of our efforts, not necessarily because of them. At colleges and universities across the nation, too often we see students seeking success at any cost, reflected in the rising tide of plagiarism and other forms of academic dishonesty. We are confronted by the loss of civility in increasingly diverse communities. We witness the feelings of fragmentation and increased psychological distress reported by campus counseling centers around the country.[2] We see a loss of balance, too often a lack of integrity, and limited vision. And yet we need all of these—balance, integrity, vision; a clear sense of collective responsibility and ethical leadership—in order to prepare our students for wise stewardship of their world and active participation in a democracy.

The technological advances of the twenty-first century will provide unanticipated opportunities for our students. They will have increasing access to ever larger quantities of information, but will they have the wisdom to use it for the common good? How do we cultivate the knowledge of self and others, the clarity of vision, the sense of perspective needed to make wise choices? Further, how do we do this in the context of ethnically and religiously diverse student communities, where we cannot assume shared cultural norms and values?

These questions are especially important in the context of a changing world order. We need an educated citizenry prepared to join an increasingly interdependent world. The American psychologist and educator John Dewey told us long ago that education could prepare people for life in a democracy only if the educational experience were also democratic. Louis Menand, in "Reimagining Liberal Education," drew from the wisdom of Dewey when he wrote, "You cannot teach people a virtue by requiring them to read books about it. You can only teach a virtue by calling upon people to exercise it. Virtue is not an innate property of character; it is an attribute of behavior."[3] We must ask if our learning environments create opportunities for practicing the behaviors required in an effective democracy.

And what is the relationship between wisdom and social justice? In my mind, you cannot have one without the other. There is no wisdom in inequity. Justice seeking requires the recognition of multiple perspectives and the opportunity for thoughtful reflection and dialogue. To quote the education leaders Lee Knefelkamp and Carol Geary Schneider,

> Justice depends on and emerges ultimately from the quality of our interactions with and sense of responsibility to other human beings. A society riven by deep divisions is hard pressed to provide meaningful justice to all its citizens. If civic relationships are characterized by segregation, strangeness, and an assumption that some of us come from cultures that are intrinsically inferior, how is it possible to respond appropriately to the moral and social circumstances of one another?[4]

Again, how do we create the opportunities for reflection, integration, and application of ideas that lead to greater self-knowledge and social understanding, that help students gain perspective and a greater recognition of the interdependence that necessarily exists within communities? What curricular and pedagogical strategies will lead us to the cultivation of wisdom? If wisdom is our goal, how can we be more intentional in our practice to facilitate its emergence? These are questions that should be at the heart of what we do as educators.

Throughout this book I have tried to suggest ways in which we are at an important historical moment with regard to education and our nation's legacy of dealing with race. It is a moment that contains both dangers and opportunities. We can allow the forces leading to greater segregation to drive us further apart as a nation; or we can use our leadership—as educators or as active citizens—to use and value higher education as a location where crucial connections can be forged. I started the book with a recounting of the drama of desegregation and now de facto resegregation that has played out in my lifetime. As the current president of a great institution of higher education who has spent a lot of time working with and studying the work of K–12 educators, I see important and overlooked connections between what happens in schools and what happens in colleges and universities. I want to end the book with some thoughts on what this historical moment means for higher education.

First, I must point out that the affirmative action era that opened the doors of historically White public and private universities in the early 1970s changed higher education significantly. For example, a sample of twenty-five selective public and private universities whose Black enrollments averaged 1.0 percent or less in 1951 had increased their share of Black undergraduates to approximately 7.0 percent by 1998.[5] One might argue whether that pace of growth in a forty-seven year period is equivalent to "all deliberate speed," but certainly it is change.

However, the retreat from school desegregation that is occurring at the K–12 level is certainly also a threat to higher education. It is a threat because both White students and students of color will come to college without the preparation that they need. Many students of color will have had reduced access to high-level college preparatory courses and the facilities that support such a curriculum. Many White students will have had less effective social preparation for diverse campus life. Further, the current legal assault on affirmative action in higher education can be seen as parallel to the resegregation of public education effected through the Supreme Court. Just as one legal case after another chipped away at the possibility of full implementation of the *Brown v. Board of Education* decision for public elementary and secondary schools, the anti–affirmative action cases directed toward higher education threaten to further the restrictions that have already been placed on special recruiting efforts and other affirmative action initiatives designed to increase the enrollment of students of color at predominantly White institutions.

Yet those of us who were the beneficiaries of *Brown,* both White and of color, and who came of age before the retrenchment of the 1990s, are now in positions of influence. We can use our spheres of influence to interrupt this backward movement. Those of us in higher education have a particular obligation to do so. The decision makers of the future are the college students of today. They need to have an understanding of the social history that has shaped their current context of racial isolation, and the choices they can make to change it.

Because of the persistence of elementary- and secondary-school segregation fifty years after the *Brown* decision, today's American youth have had few opportunities to interact with those racially, ethnically, or religiously different from them before they go to college. In a recent conversation I had with a White male colleague who lives and works in a largely White community, he lamented that his son had no Black friends, and to his dismay, his son was expressing some negative attitudes toward the African American students he did encounter. My colleague, also in his fifties, was like me a child of *Brown* who had been able to develop close cross-racial friendships in school, and he was worried that his son would not benefit from such an experience himself. His son's story illustrates well the fact that lack of direct experience means that what one learns about the "other" is too often secondhand information, conveyed in the form of media stereotypes. Even when parents have positive racial attitudes, children can absorb the prejudices of their peers and the wider cultural milieu. The specific content of those prejudices, and their targets, will vary depending on where students have grown up and what their life experience has been. But we can be sure that all members of our campus population have come to college with stereotypes and prejudices about some other segment of our student body. How could it be otherwise when there is so much misinformation circulating in the environment?

As a result, colleges, of all the institutions in our country, have some of the greatest responsibility to challenge misconceptions and explore differences—and to help our students develop their capacity to connect across them. Most of our students do not come with this capacity for connection already developed, yet it is a capacity that *can* be developed. Increasingly, educators are recognizing the need to foster this capacity as an essential outcome of a quality education. A recent study conducted by leaders at the nation's institutional accrediting bodies in conjunction with several higher education associations revealed a remarkable consensus on fifteen key outcomes that all students, regardless of major or academic background, should achieve while in college. Among them were civic responsibility and engagement, ethical reasoning, teamwork, and intercultural knowledge and actions.[6] Each of these competencies requires or is enhanced by the opportunity to engage with those whose perspectives and life experiences are different from one's own—perspectives and experiences that when shared can challenge and stimulate one's own critical thinking.

Empirical research has supported what many educators have observed through our classroom experiences about the educational benefits of learning in a diverse community.[7] Drawing on national data from colleges and universities across the country as well as from data specific to the University of Michigan, the social psychologist Pat Gurin and her colleagues concluded that those students who experienced the most racial and ethnic diversity in and out of their classrooms benefited in terms of both "learning outcomes" and "democracy outcomes."[8] Greater engagement in active thinking processes, growth in intellectual engagement and motivation, and growth in intellectual and academic skills were among the benefits to students actively involved in a diverse campus community. These students also showed the most involvement during college in various forms of citizenship, the most engagement with people from different races and cultures, and they were the most likely to acknowledge that group differences are compatible with the interests of the broader community—all outcomes important to the health of our democracy. When we consider the problems posed by the current trend of school resegregation, it is encouraging to know that students who had the most diversity experiences during college continued that pattern of cross-racial interaction—in their neighborhoods and at work —several years after their college graduation.

The last finding is a particularly powerful one in light of the self-perpetuating power of segregation in U.S. society. Those who grow up in segregated environments tend to stay in them. As Pat Gurin commented in her expert testimony in the University of Michigan affirmative action case, "If institutions of higher education are able to bring together students from various ethnic and racial backgrounds at the critical time of late adolescence and early adulthood, they have the opportunity to disrupt an insidious cycle of lifetime segregation that threatens the fabric of our pluralistic democracy."[9] These are the students—today's young college students—who have the potential to interrupt our well-established patterns of residential segregation and can perhaps begin to make the ideal of *Brown* a reality.

This may seem like an odd point for me to make, given that I am the president of Spelman College, the oldest historically Black college for women. If cross-group interaction is so important, why are Black colleges still relevant fifty years after *Brown*? For me, the answer lies in the clear pattern of resistance to desegregation. Racism (and certainly sexism) persist in ways that leave Black women (and men) on the margins of too many learning environments.

Consider this: In the summer of 2005, six young Black women represented Spelman College at the International RoboCup, an annual robotics competition in Osaka, Japan. There they competed with twenty-four other teams from around the world, including technology giants like Georgia Tech and Carnegie Mellon. The SpelBots, as the team is called, made history as the first ever all-female and all-Black team to compete in this competition. Would six Black women be leading the robotics team anywhere else? It is unlikely. In a world where, as recently as 2005, an influential educator such as Lawrence Summers, then the president of Harvard University, can publicly question the intrinsic aptitude of women to excel in science, it seems quite unlikely.[10] Yet what a fantastic opportunity it has been for young Black women from Spelman to pursue excellence in robotics and other sciences without the barrier of lowered expectations to impede them. We still need such environments where those who have been historically left out are expected and encouraged to stretch themselves to their highest potential. There is still power, and empowerment, that comes from the historically Black college experience, just as there is still power in the mentoring and leadership opportunities offered by women's colleges. At Spelman, both of these aspects of identity are affirmed for young women of African descent in a powerful way.

Another example comes from a student who sent me an e-mail message about transferring to Spelman. She wrote:

This past summer I had the opportunity to read your book *"Why Are All the Black Kids Sitting Together in the Cafeteria?"*

I was able to identify with many of the points that you made. In fact I am one of the exact products of your book. I went through the entire experience in my high school. I had what most people would have considered then to be a diverse reality; however, in many areas having a decent mix of people just wasn't enough. Our cafeteria was divided in half, with Blacks on the left and Whites on the right, and so were all of the events like games, pep rallies, etc. The Black people gathered together for many of the reasons that you discussed in your book. We were a support group, we were large enough, and we had a "voice." Many of us held positions in which we could input our ideas about policy and about administrative decisions.

However, I am now a sophomore at [a historically White college in a southern city], and I am in a similar situation. The only difference between my college and high school experience is that now I am battling segregation along with racism from the administration, faculty, and the students, while trying to obtain a degree simultaneously. The Black people who attend my school do not have a voice, and we operate on a day to day basis in an environment that is resistant to change and consciously racist. This environment has stalled my growth on many levels, and the worst part of all is that I am a Gates Millennium Scholar, meaning that I can go anywhere in the U.S. and have my tuition paid for in full. So, I am sure that you will understand me when I say that I would rather not put my scholarship money into an institution that is not facilitating my growth. All of these points bring me to my final dilemma. Everything that I lack at this institution, support as a Black female and a facilitated learning environment, I know that I can find at Spelman. I believe that I am qualified, and have a great deal to contribute to the college and community.

That student did indeed transfer successfully to Spelman. We must support those learning environments that continue to foster the achievement of those who have been historically marginalized even as we work to improve learning environments for students of color across the spectrum of education. It has been my goal throughout my career to help institutions like the one described above to become healthier places for both students of color *and* their fellow White students. That is still my goal even as I work to ensure the strength of Spelman College and other institutions like it. *It is not an "either-or" choice, it is a "both-and" solution.*

THE ABC'S OF CREATING A CLIMATE OF ENGAGEMENT

I want to come back to the ABC's of creating inclusive environments that I described in Chapter 1—affirming identity, building community, and cultivating leadership, three critical dimensions of effective learning environments in which students feel invested and engaged, not just during the college years but through all levels of education.

AFFIRMING IDENTITY. As noted in Chapter 1, it is often harder for those students who have been historically marginalized in our culture to see themselves reflected positively in school. This continues to be true at many predominantly White colleges and universities, and the demand for ethnic studies courses on campuses around the United States can be understood in part as a need for one's presence to be acknowledged in the institution. The establishment of cultural centers is another common approach to addressing the need to affirm marginalized identities on predominantly White campuses. Along with the specialized programming that is often based in such centers, they provide a physical location to which students can briefly retreat from campus environments that, despite an institution's best efforts, are alienating at times.

BUILDING COMMUNITY. Students also need to sense that they belong to a larger, shared campus community, and some observers argue that while the existence of cultural centers and related programs affirm identity, they work against building community, encouraging separation rather than the cross-group engagement we seek. As paradoxical as it may seem, the opposite is more often the case. Students who feel that their own needs for affirmation have been met are more willing and able to engage with others across lines of difference. When an important need is met, we don't have to spend energy pursuing it. Rather we can use our energy to push ourselves academically and socially. Most of us are more willing to engage in the often-taxing work of crossing social borders when we are operating from strength. Affirming identity is not contradictory to but a prerequisite for building community. Learning to build community, to think inclusively, to cross borders, is both a challenge and a benefit of being part of a diverse campus community.

The challenge at many institutions is that there are not enough structured opportunities for the affirmation of identity or for border-crossing conversations to take place. Interestingly, cultural centers can serve both purposes. For example, when my oldest son was a freshman at Wesleyan University, he chose to live in the Malcolm X House, a cultural center with residential capacity for about thirty students. At the end of his first year, in the spring of 2001, he asked me if I would come to Wesleyan to facilitate a dialogue, not for the Black students alone, but a campus-wide dialogue to be held at the Malcolm X House. I tried to talk him out of it, because it was the end of the semester and I imagined that everyone would be studying for exams and there would be limited participation. He assured me that it was very important to him, and that he was confident that the gathering would be well attended. I agreed to come, and indeed my son was right. The large lounge in the Malcolm X House was packed with a very diverse group of students. Clearly they were hungry for dialogue, and the Malcolm X House was the perfect place for it to happen. For some White students, it probably felt like entering foreign territory, but it provided the opportunity to risk some discomfort in a way that could foster the kind of growth that Gurin and her colleagues described. And a larger sense of shared purpose was emerging through their dialogue—they were building a multiracial community.

Although during the conversation some White students questioned the value of cultural centers like the Malcolm X House, I thought about what a benefit it had been to my son, who had grown up in a predominantly White community, to have the opportunity to immerse himself in the social milieu of the house, even as he continued to experience the mostly White learning environment of his daily coursework. *Because* of his experience in the Malcolm X House, not in spite of it, he was getting exactly what he wanted and needed during that first year at Wesleyan. As his own needs for affirmation were met, he began to emerge as a leader in the larger campus community. Organizing the year-end dialogue was just one manifestation of that developing leadership. Although I did not have the opportunity for follow-up conversations with the White students at Wesleyan, one of my former students at Mount Holyoke College shared these reflections about her ventures into campus spaces where she was in the minority:

> Many people on campus feel like events hosted [by students of color] are only for those who identify with that group. I too used to think this, but now I know the community is always

welcome to attend any event. Although I was at first hesitant to show up at a cultural house, this semester I have attended several social events there. I had a great time.... Although as a White woman, I will never know how it feels to be a minority, I was certainly not in the majority at [the Black student cultural center]....I now feel more at ease at these parties. Likewise, I believe cultural houses help women of color to feel more at ease on [our] campus....I used to think because I was not affiliated with the group who maintains the house that I was not welcome. Cultural centers represent an important educational site for White students. All students should take advantage of the excellent opportunity cultural houses provide to rid them of fear.

Creating opportunities to master one's fear of difference should be a part of the college experience, and that can happen at any kind of institution.

CULTIVATING LEADERSHIP. Leadership in the twenty-first century not only requires the ability to think critically and speak and write effectively, it also demands the ability to interact effectively with others from different backgrounds. The development of each of these abilities requires opportunities to practice. The Intergroup Relations (IGR) Program at the University of Michigan is an excellent model of one successful strategy. This multifaceted program offers a course for first-year students that incorporates five key conditions: the presence of diverse others, a change from pre-college experiences, equality among peers, discussion under guidelines of civil discourse, and normalization and negotiation of conflict. In addition to the usual lectures, readings, and papers, the students participate in face-to-face intergroup dialogues. Heterogeneous groups of students are brought together to engage one another in active discussion of often controversial topics, confronting multiple points of view in the process, and fostering the capacity for the perspective-taking needed for collaborative problem-solving.[11] The student facilitators who are trained to lead these discussion groups emerge with a sophisticated understanding of group dynamics and well-honed leadership abilities. Everyone benefits from the practice.

FROM THEORY TO PRACTICE

Whether at a historically Black college or a predominantly White institution, we all must ask ourselves, "How do we create and sustain educational environments that affirm identity, build community, and cultivate leadership in ways that support the learning of all students?" Translating the ABC's into action requires us to routinely ask one another important questions: Who is reflected in our environment? Who is missing from the picture? What opportunities exist for building community, for encouraging dialogue across difference? How are students involved so that they are honing leadership skills in a diverse context?

At Spelman, though 97 percent of our students are racially categorized as "Black," the student body is, in fact, quite diverse. Spelman students come from all regions of the United States and many foreign countries, from White suburban and rural communities as well as urban Black ones. All parts of the African Diaspora are represented, and the variety of experience and perspectives among the women who attend the college creates many opportunities for important dialogue. There is a developmental moment in the lives of young people of color when "within group" dialogue can be as important, or perhaps even sometimes more important, than "between group" dialogue.

And, even in the context of a historically Black college, it is possible to create opportunities for both.

For example, at Spelman, an institution with deep Christian roots, I acknowledge the significant presence of Muslim students on our campus by cohosting with the Dean of the Chapel an iftar (a "break the fast" meal) during Ramadan for Muslim faculty, students, staff, and their guests. We have developed a program for interfaith dialogue as a way to address the religious diversity within our population of Black students, and have created occasional opportunities for interethnic dialogue among African, African American, and Afro-Caribbean students through our Center for Leadership and Civic Engagement. For many years, the Spelman College Women's Research and Resource Center has been a location on campus that fosters important and challenging conversations about racial and gender equity, heterosexism and homophobia, and the role of Black women as agents of change, through coursework, featured guest speakers, and workshops throughout the year. These few examples illustrate multiple points of entry—curricular and cocurricular—into conversations that will help students challenge their own assumptions and help prepare them for leadership in a diverse world.

In our efforts to foster student capacity to connect with others across lines of difference as a critical component of leadership development, we must remember that timing is important. Our students will need time to practice these skills—and their time with us is short, which means we should begin from the moment they arrive on campus. Orientation is a natural starting point, as new students are meeting one another and also learning about the values of the institution. If inclusive values are important, that should be apparent from the very beginning.

For example, when I served as dean at Mount Holyoke College, I had oversight of our orientation planning. My staff and I struggled to bring together a diverse group of first-year students, many of whom were international students. We wanted to both affirm the identities of students who literally came from all over the world, and also build a shared sense of community. We experimented with asking students to bring something from home that represented their culture to be used in a small group exercise on the first day of orientation. We learned however that some White students from the United States were completely stumped by this request because they believed they did not have a culture. They could see that students of color and international students had a culture to share, but their own culture was invisible to them. If we are to engage with one another as equals, we all have to have something to bring to the table—and surprisingly, some White students did not feel they had anything to bring.

With this in mind, the following year we tried a different approach—a poetry exercise developed by the educator Linda Christensen that can be done with little advance preparation.[12] Using the stem "I am from" for each stanza, we asked students to describe familiar items found around their homes, sights, sounds, and smells from their neighborhoods, names of foods and dishes enjoyed at special family gatherings, familiar family sayings, and names of relatives or other important people who are a link to their past. The act of writing the poems helped to make each student's culture visible, not only to others but also to herself. To illustrate this exercise, here are some sample verses of my own poem:

I am from books, books, and more books,
long afternoons spent at the library,
traveling way beyond the limits of my small town.

I am from stone walls, and dairy farms,
brilliant autumn leaves and church school hayrides,
the sound of my brother's saxophone at 5 a.m.,
and the cheers of the Saturday afternoon football crowd
    across the street.

I am from tofu balls and biscuits, grits and eggs
pancakes every Saturday,
coconut cake on my birthday,
and pizza, pizza and more pizza if J. T. has his way.

I am from "Treat people the way you want to be treated,"
"If you don't have something nice to say, don't say
    anything at all,"
and "We are pleased but not surprised" when I share
    good news.
I am from "Eat your vegetables" but *not* the lima beans!

I am from Hazel and Maxwell, Bob and Catherine,
Victor Hugo and Constance Eleanor
a long line of educators,
I am from proud men and women working for change.

After writing their poems, an activity of about ten minutes, the students shared them in small groups of six or seven students, each group facilitated by an older student-orientation leader. Following the small-group discussion, students were invited to come forward to microphones set up around the meeting room and read their poems to their new classmates. It was exciting and inspiring to see how many students wanted to share their poems, sometimes with their papers shaking in their nervous hands, yet still stepping forward to the microphone. Although the diversity in the room was apparent, the less obvi-

121

ous similarity of experiences started to emerge as students quickly made connections to one another's lives. When given a chance to evaluate the activity later, the students' comments revealed what had been learned: "Even White suburbia has culture"; "Although we have a lot of differences, we also have many things in common. This is an amazing group of people!" Embedded in this activity were all three of the ABC's—affirming the identities of each woman as she read her poem, building community as they found common ground, and cultivating leadership of the student volunteers who honed their facilitation skills in this very diverse context.

Sometimes we allow students to wait too late to partake of what we are offering them. As dean, I often met with seniors who were trying to make sure they had taken all the required courses needed for graduation. I observed to my disappointment that some of the seniors I talked to had waited until the last semester of their senior year to satisfy the "multicultural" requirement. Although the requirement was broadly defined to include a wide variety of courses focused on people of color in the United States or in Africa, Asia, Latin America, or the Middle East, some students seemed to have delayed as long as they possibly could before exploring this new territory. My concern about this delay was that if you wait until your senior year to broaden your perspective in this way, you lose the opportunity for your new learning to inform your interaction with your fellow students over an extended time. Wouldn't it be better if students could get exposed to multicultural perspectives in their first year, perhaps as part of a first-year seminar, so that their new learning might help provide context for the interactions they would have with students from the communities about which they were learning?

I tested this idea of early intervention in my own teaching by shifting the enrollment from seniors to sophomores in my

Psychology of Racism course, a popular elective course that I taught for many years. Because the course was often oversubscribed, I had given preference to seniors, recognizing that it might be their last opportunity to take it. But when I started giving priority to sophomores instead, the benefit of the course to the campus community increased. The sophomores who emerged from the course with a better understanding of the historical context of racism and the meaning of racial identity in a race-conscious society were able to use that understanding in their interactions with fellow students in ways that positively impacted the campus. These were the students who initiated dialogue groups on campus, brought a multicultural perspective to their student organizations, and began to expand their own horizons by seeking out friendship networks more diverse than those they had before taking the course, and still had two more years to practice those skills before they moved on to the next phase of their lives. Courses that actively encourage cross-group dialogue can be very useful, but they need to happen early in the young person's college experience for maximum benefit.

A great example of a first-year seminar that affirms identity, builds community, and cultivates leadership is the African Diaspora and the World (ADW) course at Spelman. Established in 1992 as a writing-intensive seminar required for all first-year students, its creation was a faculty-directed effort to reimagine the World Civilization (History) and World Literature (English) core course requirements in ways that would (1) place the African Diaspora at the center of the student's sociohistorical, literary, and cultural studies; (2) reflect the shifting demographics of the United States and the world; and (3) prepare Spelman women for a new era of diversity and global interaction. Described in the Spelman course catalog as a two-semester course that "seeks to examine the major themes

123

associated with the African Diaspora within a global context and from perspectives that are both interdisciplinary and gender-informed," ADW is now a signature course at Spelman, considered by many Spelman students to be one of their most powerful and personally defining educational experiences at the college.

A foundational course that speaks to the identity issues that motivated many of them to choose Spelman College, ADW is frequently the one course that alumnae say has most influenced both their career success and dedication to promoting social justice. It connects directly to the Spelman College mission of "empowering the total person," who not only understands and appreciates the many cultures of the world, but also has a deeper understanding of her own and other cultures of Africa and its Diaspora.

The connection to identity is clear, but it also builds community as a shared intellectual experience, and helps students to understand the diversity within the Spelman community, as our students represent various communities of the African Diaspora. As their understanding of their global awareness expands, their capacity for leadership is enhanced.

As curricular and programmatic innovation is considered, we must also remember that this is not work that can be done well quickly. You can't bring a complex conversation about race to closure in the two hours of a single afternoon workshop, or even a whole day of resident adviser (RA) orientation. Too often what is accomplished in that period of time is just enough to generate anxiety, and anxiety often leads to avoidance. Put simply, "I don't want to talk about it" becomes a common response. An article I wrote in 1992 describes the emotional responses that students, both White students and students of color, are likely to have to race-related information, and what we can do to keep them in the dialogue long enough to get to the place where they actually feel the benefit of the conversation.[13] Trying to shortcut the process is a bit like treating a child for an ear infection. The doctor will tell you to give the child antibiotics for seven days, but after the second day of medication, the child's ear feels better and the child's fussing is no longer about the pain in his ear but about the taste of the medicine. There's a temptation to stop giving the medicine—after all, the child feels better. But if you don't give the whole prescription, the ear infection will return and it will come back more virulently. And the next time that antibiotic is not going to work at all. Diversity training, or antiracism training, can be like that. If you just give a little dose, you simply build up resistance. You have to give enough to make some real progress, to get past the initial discomfort, and persist to the point where you can really begin to see the benefits.

If we really want to have these conversations, and have them in ways that help us, it has to be an ongoing dialogue. It is one reason that I recommend the framework of a course as one strategy—a semester includes adequate time to provide context for important social issues, an opportunity to explore the individual and societal implications of the issue, and even help students strategize about what they can do to effect change.

It may seem that implied in these comments is the assumption that we—faculty, staff, administrators—know how to facilitate these conversations ourselves. The reality is that a lot of us don't. But we can learn. And we can support one another in the process. When I first began teaching about racism in 1980 I was a novice instructor, and I know I made mistakes. But even in my inexperienced state, my students told me that I was changing their lives by giving them permission to talk about race—powerful feedback for a then twenty-six-year old instructor! That conversation is still needed, perhaps more now than ever.

Although some progress has been made, the road to racial equality is not complete, and it appears that some have abandoned the task. But as a child of *Brown,* I know that change is possible, even if it is sometimes slow and not easily made permanent. My father could not attend the graduate school of his choice. His daughter did, as did his grandson. *More* change is still needed. As the door of school desegregation closes, perhaps a new door of dialogue-driven action can open, enabling us to build bridges across divided communities and meet the educational needs of all of our students. We owe it to ourselves and the generations that follow us to try. *Can we talk about race?*

AFTERWORD
THERESA PERRY

Can we reclaim the grand idea—if flawed in initial conception and implementation—of schools as the great equalizer? Will we take the time to understand the role that race has and continues to play in determining who has access to what kind of education?

The Problem We All Live With. This is the title of a documentary film that a group of students from Boston's Brighton High School produced in 2004. Graphically and in a dramatic fashion, the students do a comparative analysis of the differences between the education they receive in their city school and the education available to their overwhelmingly White counterparts in a suburban high school. In the film, we are given a tour of a decaying Boston high school, with paint peeling off the walls, leaking roofs, small, dark, and unattractive classrooms. We also see the light, airy, spacious classrooms and facilities of the suburban high school. While the differences in facilities, visually observed, are arresting, what is more affecting are the voices of students, the White students from the suburban school and the Black and Latino students from the city school, as they describe and theorize about the reasons for the discrepancies in curricula, resources, teacher expectations, and support available in the two environments. After you have watched the presentation, it is hard to get out of your mind the plaintive voice of a Black male from the city school as he talks about wanting to enroll in an honors algebra class and twice being closed out because of limited space. His comment is positioned alongside that of a suburban White student who, in her privileged environment, rattles off quickly—as if to suggest that so much is available that she might miss something if she goes slowly—the range and diversity of course offerings, in addition to numerous honors and AP classes in virtually all content areas.

A *Boston Globe* article from November 26, 2006 (Tracy Jan, "School Makeovers, Fueled by Middle Class") focused on White middle-class parents, some of whom were registering for their neighborhood schools as a group and raising money for their respective schools once their children had enrolled. One group of parents had raised $90,000 to expand the activities, offerings, and budget of their local school. The article's focus was on the benefits of bringing White middle-class parents back into the Boston public schools, while briefly alluding to the issues that might arise from this fund-raising activity; that is, the White parents having too much control and power at the schools. Neither the article nor the subsequent letters to the editor focused on the questions this scenario raises about the public's commitment to equal educational opportunity, about our contemporary vision of public education, and how race figures into this vision.

In 2005, in *Hancock et al. v. Commissioner of Education,* a case emblematic of school financing and equalization lawsuits across the country, the Supreme Judicial Court of Massachusetts rejected the claim, brought on behalf of students from nineteen school districts, that the state was not meeting its constitutional responsibility to provide equitable funding for an adequate education for children from the low-wealth school districts. In a 5–2 ruling against the plaintiff class, the justices noted, "A system mired in failure has given way to one that, although far from perfect, shows a steady trajectory of progress." "Progress" was the watchword, not "equal educational opportunity." Essentially, the court allowed the government to back away from its responsibility to provide equal educational opportunity for all students. (See Cindy Roy, Michael P. Norton, and Amy Lambiasa, "SJC Applauds Education Improvements, Rejects Hancock Case Plaintiffs," *State House News,* February 15, 2005.)

Charter school advocates—business leaders, policymakers, and educators—extol the virtues of charter schools as an option for the children and youth of urban America. And yet, throughout the country, some of the buildings in which these schools are housed would be considered unacceptable learning environments for children in middle- and high-income school districts. Some charter schools are devoid of gyms, science labs, auditoriums, libraries—all the facilities that African Americans in their historic struggle for equal educational opportunity demanded and often financed themselves when state and local funding was not forthcoming. Has personal choice replaced both the collective demand and the public will for equal educational opportunity for all? A group of Black middle school students in Atlanta provided an apt commentary on the conditions of the charter schools that they and their friends were attending, calling them "bootleg schools."

From Baltimore, Maryland, to Los Angeles, California, Black and Latino students are demanding AP and honors classes, clean bathrooms, up-to-code buildings, books, universal access to a college preparatory curriculum, teachers who hold high expectations of them, and more. Even as these youth engage in struggles for equal educational opportunity, for quality education as a civil right, an ideological discourse holds sway in the public domain that blames these students, their

129

peer groups, their parents, and their communities for their underperformance in school.

In the midst of shameful educational inequities and against the backdrop of a public discourse that foregrounds progress and accountability while inequality of educational resources remains unaddressed; in the midst of a reemergence of theories of cultural deficiency as an explanation for school failure while a new generation of youth struggles for a right to quality education; can we re-envision public schools as the great equalizer? What conversations do we need to have about race, education, and democracy in order for this view of schools to take hold? What do we need to know about our present, about the past, about how race historically undermined and continues to undermine the necessary link between education, citizenship, and the possibility of a robust democracy?

In the spring of 2006, Simmons College and Beacon Press, two distinguished Boston institutions, entered into a collaborative relationship and launched the Simmons College/Beacon Press Race, Education, and Democracy lecture and book series. We wanted to provide a public location for ordinary citizens, individuals from many walks of life and from different racial and ethnic backgrounds, to begin to have the conversations necessary to rearticulate a vision of public schools as a common good, as the great equalizer, and of quality education as a civil right. And we wanted these lectures to have a life beyond their occurrences, one that would be captured in short, accessible, general-interest books that could inspire further reflection, dialogue, and action.

In pursuit of these goals, each year, the Simmons College/ Beacon Press series will select a prominent scholar to deliver four or five public lectures on the topic of race, education, and democracy. We are gratified that Dr. Beverly Daniel Tatum, the ninth president of Spelman College and the author of the highly acclaimed book *"Why Are All the Black Kids Sitting To-gether in the Cafeteria?" And Other Conversations about Race* agreed to give the inaugural lectures in the series. While we knew that members of the general public were deeply inter-ested in the issue of race and its impact on education, the pub-lic's response to the 2006 lecture series, to both the topic and to Dr. Tatum, was overwhelming, with more than seven hundred individuals attending the lectures. And the audience was as diverse as we imagined, with attendees representing the rich racial and ethnic diversity that characterizes the Boston area and including high school students, graduate students, com-munity and religious leaders, policymakers, activists, teachers and principals, elected officials, school board members, college professors, and retirees.

This book is based on those public lectures. In it Dr. Tatum opens exactly the kind of conversation we need so urgently to have about education, race, and the American community. She asks us, in particular, to talk about race in an era of the reseg-regation of public schools, and her range of topics throughout the book shows the complexity of the terrain—from issues of identity and achievement to the possibilities of cross-racial friendship to the responsibilities of higher education. She asks us to understand how race and decisions informed by racial understandings have contributed to the resegregation of the schools. In a hopeful stance, she lays out throughout the book what we can do in these segregated environments to prepare students of color and White students to live and work in our multiracial, multicultural democracy. And among many other things, she profiles the promising practices of individual edu-cators and public school systems in these challenging times.

We are pleased to present this book as the first in the Sim-mons College/Beacon Press Race, Education, and Democracy series. It is our hope that it challenges its readers to talk about race in more complicated ways. It is our hope that this book will help individuals reclaim Horace Mann's vision of schools as the great equalizer and spur us on to commit ourselves to make sure that our educational institutions—public schools, colleges, and universities—become laboratories for a democracy predicated on difference, laboratories for a multiracial, multicultural democracy. Can we talk about race, education, and democracy?

THERESA PERRY is a professor in the departments of Africana Studies and Education at Simmons College and director of the Simmons College/Beacon Press Race, Education, and Democracy lecture and book series. She is coauthor, with Asa Hilliard III and Claude Steele, of *Young, Gifted, and Black: Promoting High Achievement among African-American Students;* coeditor, with Lisa Delpit, of *The Real Ebonics Debate: Power, Language, and the Education of African-American Children;* editor of *Teaching Malcolm X;* and coeditor of *Freedom's Plow: Teaching in the Multicultural Classroom.*

ACKNOWLEDGMENTS

Although the essays presented here are based on four lectures given at Simmons College in the spring of 2006, they represent many conversations held with students and colleagues over a number of years. I have been privileged to spend a lifetime with brilliant students, and many years with dedicated educators who are committed to antiracist classroom practices, and I have learned a great deal from the examples they shared and the questions they asked. I thank them all.

This collection would not have been possible without the invitation of Dr. Theresa Perry of Simmons College and the encouragement and helpful editing of Andy Hrycyna of Beacon Press. It is hard to fit the production of a book into the schedule of a college president and I often wondered if it was possible. But as I worked on the book it became very clear to me that it was important to find the time.

Many projects begin, but no project ends, without the love and support of my husband, Travis Tatum, carrying me through. He reads every word as many times as I need, and he always has something helpful to say. I am truly blessed. To my parents, Robert and Catherine Daniel, I know you are pleased but not surprised. Thank you for your unending support and encouragement. To Travis, Jonathan, David, and Shanesha, thank you for your patience at Thanksgiving as I pressed toward my deadline. I know you will carry the torch for the next generation.

At Spelman College we have a compelling mission to develop the intellectual, ethical, and leadership potential of our students. Spelman seeks to empower the total person, who appreciates the many cultures of the world and commits to positive social change.

I find inspiration in that mission every day. As we celebrate 125 years of educating women who change the world, I want to thank the Spelman College community for allowing me to serve as their leader during this important time in the life of the college.

When Coretta Scott King received her honorary degree from Spelman in 1984, she left us with these words:

> Yes, as graduates you can be proud of a remarkable heritage of achievement. However, I know you won't rest on your laurels too long, because this great heritage means you also have a responsibility. You have an awesome responsibility to pick up the burden of leadership which rightfully falls to the educated Black woman. No matter what kind of career you are planning, you are challenged to be a leader—not just a leader in your chosen profession, but a leader of the struggle for economic and social justice, and for world peace. You also have a very special responsibility to other Black women, particularly those who have not had the opportunity to get a decent education. The tragic social and economic conditions being forced on millions of our sisters is a national disgrace. If you, as educated Black women, don't accept the responsibility for providing the kind of leadership to correct these injustices, then who will?

I acknowledge this responsibility, and I thank Mrs. King for the clarity of her charge.

NOTES

INTRODUCTION: CAN WE TALK ABOUT RACE?

1. The Michigan Civil Rights Initiative was approved by Michigan voters in the November 2006 election.

2. See Linda Darling-Hammond, "The Right to Learn and the Advancement of Teaching: Research, Policy, and Practice for Democratic Education," *Educational Researcher* 25, no. 6 (1996), 5–17.

3. See Harry G. Lefever, *Undaunted by the Fight: Spelman College and the Civil Rights Movement, 1957–1967* (Macon, Ga.: Mercer University Press, 2005), 27–30.

4. Beverly Daniel Tatum, *"Why Are All the Black Kids Sitting Together in the Cafeteria?"; and Other Conversations about Race* (New York: Basic Books, 1997).

5. For an expanded discussion of racial and ethnic categories, see Chapters 1 and 8 in Tatum, *"Why Are All the Black Kids Sitting Together in the Cafeteria?"*

6. See John Charles Boger and Gary Orfield, eds., *School Resegregation: Must the South Turn Back?* (Chapel Hill: University of North Carolina Press, 2005).

7. For a summary of the educational history of Native Americans and Asian Americans in the United States, see Joel Spring, *Deculturalization and the Struggle for Equality: A Brief History of the Education of Dominated Cultures in the United States,* 2nd ed. (New York: McGraw-Hill, 1997). For a discussion of the experiences of more recent Asian immigrants, see Stacey J. Lee, *Up Against*

Whiteness: Race, School, and Immigrant Youth (New York: Teachers College Press, 2005).

8. Thomas Friedman, *The World Is Flat: A Brief History of the Twenty-first Century* (New York: Farrar, Straus and Giroux, 2005).

CHAPTER ONE: THE RESEGREGATION OF OUR SCHOOLS AND THE AFFIRMATION OF IDENTITY

1. Charles Clotfelter, *After Brown: The Rise and Retreat of School Desegregation* (Princeton, N.J.: Princeton University Press, 2004), 16–17.

2. Ibid., 14.

3. Ibid., 19.

4. Joel H. Spring, *Deculturalization and the Struggle for Equality: A Brief History of the Education of Dominated Cultures in the United States,* 3rd ed. (Boston: McGraw-Hill, 2001).

5. *Brown v. Board of Education II,* 349 U.S. 294 (1955), italics mine.

6. Charles J. Ogletree Jr., *All Deliberate Speed: Reflections on the First Half Century of Brown v. Board of Education* (New York: Norton, 2004), 10.

7. See Peter Irons, *Jim Crow's Children: The Broken Promise of the Brown Decision* (New York: Viking, 2002).

8. Ibid., 204.

9. Clotfelter, *After Brown,* 26–27.

10. F. A. Holloway, "What Is Affirmative Action?" in *Affirmative Action in Perspective,* ed. Fletcher A. Blanchard and Faye A. Crosby (New York: Springer-Verlag, 1989), 9–19; Dalmas Taylor, "Affirmative Action and Presidential Executive Orders," in *Affirmative Action in Perspective,* ed. Blanchard and Crosby, 21–29.

11. Faye J. Crosby, "Understanding Affirmative Action," *Basic and Applied Social Psychology* 15, nos. 1 and 2 (April 1994), 13–41.

12. For an expanded discussion of affirmative action, see Beverly Daniel Tatum, *"Why Are All the Black Kids Sitting Together in the Cafeteria?"; and Other Conversations about Race,* rev. ed. (New York: Basic Books, 2003), 114–28.

13. See Clotfelter, *After Brown,* 188.

14. For a discussion of W. E. B. DuBois's concept of the talented tenth and the double consciousness of African Americans, see his classic text, *The Souls of Black Folk,* originally published in 1903 (New York: Signet Books, 1969).

15. William E. Cross Jr., *Shades of Black: Diversity in African-American identity* (Philadelphia: Temple University Press, 1991).

16. Gary Orfield, Susan E. Eaton, and the Harvard Project on School Desegregation, *Dismantling Desegregation: The Quiet Reversal of Brown v. Board of Education* (New York: New Press, 1996).

17. As cited in Clotfelter, *After Brown,* 30–31.

18. *Milliken v. Bradley,* 418 U.S. 717 (1974).

19. Irons, *Jim Crow's Children,* 257.

20. *Board of Education of Oklahoma City v. Dowell,* 498 U.S. 237 (1991).

21. Irons, *Jim Crow's Children,* 259–71.

22. Ibid., 271.

23. John Charles Boger and Gary Orfield, eds., *School Resegregation: Must the South Turn Back?* (Chapel Hill: University of North Carolina Press, 2005), 3.

24. U.S. Census Bureau, Population Estimates Program, July 1, 2004. The census now allows respondents to identify more than one racial group. The data are reported in terms of "single race" as well as "one race in combination with one or more races." I have used the percentages for "single race" in this summary.

25. John Logan et al., *Ethnic Diversity Grows, Neighborhood Integration Lags Behind* (Albany, N.Y.: Lewis Mumford Center for Comparative Urban and Regional Research, April 2001), http://mumford.albany.edu/census/WholePop/WPreport/page1.html.

26. Thomas W. Sanchez, Rich Stolz, and Jacinta S. Ma, *Moving to Equity: Addressing Inequitable Effects of Transportation Policies on Minorities* (Cambridge, Mass.: Civil Rights Project, Harvard University; Washington, D.C.: Center for Community Change, 2003).

27. john a. powell, "True Integration," in *School Resegregation*, ed. Boger and Orfield, 284.

28. As cited in Clotfelter, *After Brown,* 181.
29. Ibid., 192.
30. Boger and Orfield, ed., *School Resegregation,* 20.
31. Ibid., 314.
32. Marilyn Cochran-Smith, *Walking the Road: Race, Diversity, and Social Justice in Teacher Education* (New York: Teachers College Press), 7.
33. Boger and Orfield, ed., *School Resegregation,* 314.
34. For an extended discussion of the legal status of race-conscious policies in K–12 public schools, see Jacinta S. Ma and Michal Kurlander, "The Future of Race-Conscious Policies in K–12 Public Schools," in *School Resegregation,* ed. Boger and Orfield, 239–60.
35. Maria Sacchetti, "Concerns Raised about Recruiting," Boston Globe, August 23, 2005.
36. *Grutter v. Bollinger,* 539 U.S. 306 (2003).
37. *Gratz v. Bollinger,* 539 U.S. 244 (2003).
38. Ma and Kurlander, "The Future of Race-Conscious Policies," 247.
39. One amicus brief of social science research, developed by researchers at the Harvard Civil Rights Project, was signed by 553 scholars, representing 201 institutions and forty-two states and the District of Columbia (www.civilrightsproject.harvard.edu/research/deseg/amicus_parents_v_seattle.pdf).
40. Susan Leigh Flinspach and Karen E. Banks, "Moving Beyond Race: Socioeconomic Diversity as a Race-Neutral Approach to Desegregation in the Wake County Schools," in *School Resegregation,* ed. Boger and Orfield, 261–80.
41. *Discrimination in Metropolitan Housing Markets: National Results from Phase 1, Phase 2, and Phase 3 of the Housing Discrimination Study (HDS),* www.huduser.org/publications/hsgfin/hds.html#newtop.
42. For several years I had the opportunity to work with teachers in several Massachusetts school districts who were actively working to develop antiracist classroom practices to benefit all of their students. Some of the work they did has been described in the following articles: Sandra M. Lawrence and Beverly Daniel Tatum,

"White Educators as Allies: Moving from Awareness to Action," in *Off White: Readings on Race, Power, and Society,* ed. Michele Fine et al. (New York: Routledge, 1997), 333–42; Beverly Daniel Tatum and Elizabeth Knaplund, "Outside the Circle? The Relational Implications for White Women Working against Racism," Work in Progress no. 78 (Wellesley, Mass.: Stone Center Working Paper Series); Beverly Daniel Tatum, "Teaching White Students about Racism: The Search for White Allies and the Restoration of Hope," *Teachers College Record* 95, no. 4 (1994): 462–76; Irwin Blumer and Beverly Daniel Tatum, "Creating a Community of Allies: How One School System Attempted to Create an Anti-Racist Environment," *International Journal of Leadership in Education* 2, no. 3 (1999): 255–67.

43. Some excellent resources include Louise Derman-Sparks, Patricia G. Ramsey, Julie Olson Edward, *What If All the Kids Are White? Anti-Bias Multicultural Education with Young Children and Families* (New York: Teachers College Press, 2006); *Rethinking Our Classrooms: Teaching for Equity and Justice,* vols. 1 and 2 (Milwaukee: Rethinking Schools, 2001).

44. Jonathan Kozol, *Savage Inequalities: Children in America's Schools* (New York: Crown, 1991).

45. Gloria Ladson-Billings, *The Dreamkeepers: Successful Teachers of African American Children* (San Francisco: Jossey-Bass, 1994); Michele Foster, *Black Teachers on Teaching* (New York: New Press,1997), Asa G. Hilliard III, "No Mystery: Closing the Achievement Gap," in *Young, Gifted, and Black: Promoting High Achievement among African-American students,* ed. Theresa Perry, Claude Steele, and Asa Hilliard III (Boston: Beacon Press, 2003).

46. Theresa Perry, "Freedom for Literacy," in *Young, Gifted, and Black: Promoting High Achievement among African-American students,* ed. Theresa Perry, Claude Steele, and Asa Hilliard III (Boston: Beacon Press, 2003), 50.

47. Vanessa Siddle Walker, *Their Highest Potential: An African American School Community in the Segregated South* (Chapel Hill: University of North Carolina Press, 1996).

48. Stephen D. Hancock, "White Women's Work: On the Front Lines in Urban Education," in *White Teachers, Diverse Classrooms,* ed. Julie Landsman and Chance W. Lewis (Sterling, Va.: Stylus, 2006), 93–109.

49. Gloria Ladson-Billings, "Landing on the Wrong Note: The Price We Paid for Brown," *Educational Researcher* 33, no. 7 (2004): 3–13.

50. Cochran-Smith, *Walking the Road,* 5.

51. Ibid., 108.

52. Hancock, "White Women's Work," 95.

53. Ladson-Billings, *The Dreamkeepers.*

54. Catherine E. Freeman, Benjamin Scafidi, and David L. Sjoquist, "Racial Segregation in Georgia Public Schools, 1994–2001: Trends, Causes and Impact on Teacher Quality," in *School Resegregation: Must the South Turn Back?* ed. John Charles Boger and Gary Orfield (Chapel Hill: University of North Carolina Press, 2005), 148–63.

55. The words to this song were written by James Weldon Johnson in 1899. The music to which it is sung was written by his brother, John R. Johnson.

56. Raymond J. Wlodkowski and Margery B. Ginsberg, *Diversity & Motivation: Culturally Responsive Teaching* (San Francisco: Jossey-Bass, 1995), 2.

57. Herbert Kohl, "I Won't Learn from You: Confronting Student Resistance," in *Rethinking Our Classrooms: Teaching for Equity and Justice* (Milwaukee: Rethinking Schools, 1994), 134–35.

58. Ibid., 135.

59. Jean Baker Miller, "Connections, Disconnections, and Violations," Work in Progress no. 33 (Wellesley, Mass.: Stone Center Working Paper Series, 1988).

60. Quoted in Sonia Nieto, *The Light in Their Eyes: Creating Multicultural Learning Communities* (New York: Teachers College Press, 1999), 85.

61. For an elaborated discussion of their response to this new content, see Beverly Daniel Tatum, "Talking about Race, Learning

about Racism: The Application of Racial Identity Development in the Classroom," *Harvard Educational Review* 62, no. 1 (1992): 1–24.

62. For an extended discussion of this point, see James Loewen, *Lies My Teacher Told Me: Everything Your American History Textbook Got Wrong* (New York: Simon and Schuster, 1995).

63. Frances E. Kendall, *Understanding White Privilege: Creating Pathways to Authentic Relationships across Race* (New York: Routledge, 2006), 82.

64. Ibid., 85.

65. For an extended discussion of White identity development, see Tatum, *"Why Are All the Black Kids Sitting Together in the Cafeteria?"* 93–113.

CHAPTER TWO: CONNECTING THE DOTS: HOW RACE IN AMERICA'S CLASSROOMS AFFECTS ACHIEVEMENT

1. See Chapter 1 in this volume.

2. For an in-depth discussion of the origin of this idea in American educational psychology, see Stephen Jay Gould, "The Hereditarian Theory of I.Q.: An American Invention," in *The Mismeasure of Man,* rev. ed. (New York: Norton, 1996), 176–263.

3. Jeff Howard, *Getting Smart: The Social Construction of Intelligence* (Waltham, Mass.: Efficacy Institute, 1992).

4. See Gould, *The Mismeasure of Man,* 178–88.

5. Ibid., 176–83.

6. Ibid., 188–89.

7. Ibid., 188–94.

8. See Leila Zenderland, *Measuring Minds: Henry Herbert Goddard and the Origins of American Intelligence Testing* (Cambridge and New York: Cambridge University Press, 1998), 267–68

9. H. H. Goddard, "The Binet Tests as Related to Immigration," *Journal of Psycho-Athenics* 18 (1913), 105–7, as cited in Gould, *The Mismeasure of Man,* 195.

10. Gould, *The Mismeasure of Man,* 196.

11. H. H. Goddard, "Mental Tests and the Immigrant," *Journal of*

Delinquency 2 (1917), 271, as cited in Gould, *The Mismeasure of Man,* 197.

12. H. H. Goddard, "Mental Tests and the Immigrant," *Journal of Delinquency* 2 (1928), 271, as cited in Gould, *The Mismeasure of Man,* 198.

13. Gould, *The Mismeasure of Man,* 207.

14. Lewis M. Terman, *The Measurement of Intelligence* (Boston: Houghton Mifflin, 1916).

15. Ibid., 91–92.

16. Gould, *The Mismeasure of Man,* 224.

17. Ibid., 247–51.

18. For a much more detailed understanding of factor analysis and its limitations as used by Charles Spearman, see Gould, *The Mismeasure of Man,* Chapter 6, 264–350.

19. C. Burt, *The Backward Child,* 10–11, as cited in Gould,*The Mismeasure of Man,* 303.

20. Gould, *The Mismeasure of Man,* 304.

21. Arthur R. Jensen, "How Much Can We Boost IQ and Scholastic Achievement?" *Harvard Educational Review* 39 (1969), 1–123.

22. Richard J. Herrnstein and Charles Murray, *The Bell Curve: Intelligence and Class Structure in American Life* (New York: Free Press, 1994).

23. Gould, *The Mismeasure of Man,* 261.

24. Howard Gardner, *Frames of Mind: The Theory of Multiple Intelligences* (New York: Basic Books, 1983).

25. Jean Piaget, *The Psychology of Intelligence* (New York: Routledge, 1950).

26. Howard, *Getting Smart.*

27. Robert Rosenthal and Lenore Jacobson, *Pygmalion in the Classroom: Teacher Expectation and Pupils' Intellectual Development* (New York: Holt, Rinehart and Winston, 1968).

28. Ibid.

29. Robert Rosenthal, "Covert Communication in Classrooms, Clinics, and Courtrooms," *Eye on Psi Chi* 3, no. 1 (1998), 18–22.

30. Sandra M. Lawrence and Beverly Daniel Tatum, "Teachers in Transition: The Impact of Antiracist Professional Development on Classroom Practice," *Teachers College Record* 99, no. 1 (fall 1997), 162–78.

31. Sandra M. Lawrence and Beverly Daniel Tatum, "White Educators as Allies: Moving from Awareness to Action," in *Off White: Readings on Race, Power, and Society,* ed. Michelle Fine et al. (New York: Routledge, 1997), 340.

32. Gwendolyn M. Parker, *Trespassing: My Sojourn in the Halls of Privilege* (Boston: Houghton Mifflin, 1997), 49.

33. Theresa Perry, "Freedom for Literacy and Literacy for Freedom: The African-American Philosophy of Education," in *Young, Gifted, and Black: Promoting High Achievement among African-American Students,* ed. Theresa Perry, Claude Steele, and Asa G. Hilliard III (Boston: Beacon, 2003), 34.

34. Ibid., 37.

35. Claude M. Steele, "Thin Ice: Stereotype Threat and Black College Students," *Atlantic Monthly* (August 1999), 44–54.

36. Claude M. Steele, "A Threat in the Air: How Stereotypes Shape Intellectual Performance and Identity," *American Psychologist* 52 (1997), 613–29.

37. Steven J. Spencer, Claude M. Steele, and Diane M. Quinn, "Stereotype Threat and Women's Math Performance," *Journal of Experimental Social Psychology* 35 (1999), 4–28.

38. Steele, "A Threat in the Air."

39. Claude Steele, "Stereotype Threat and African-American Student Achievement," in *Young, Gifted, and Black*, ed. Perry, Steele, and Hilliard, 121.

40. Geoffrey L. Cohen and Claude M. Steele, "A Barrier of Mistrust: How Negative Stereotypes Affect Cross-Race Mentoring," in *Improving Academic Achievement: Impact of Psychological Factors on Education,* ed. Joshua Aronson (San Diego: Academic, 2002), 303–28.

41. Steele, "Thin Ice," 51.

42. Steele, "Stereotype Threat," 126.

43. Ibid., 126.

44. As quoted in Howard, *Getting Smart,* 12.

45. Carol Dweck, "Messages That Motivate: How Praise Molds Students' Beliefs, Motivation, and Performance (in Surprising Ways)," in *Improving Academic Achievement,* ed. Aronson, 38–60.

46. Joshua Aronson, Carrie B. Fried, and Catherine Good, "Reducing the Effects of Stereotype Threat on African American College Students by Shaping Theories of Intelligence," *Journal of Experimental Social Psychology* 38, no. 2 (2002), 1–13.

47. Lisa Sorich Blackwell, Kali Trzesniewski, and Carol Dweck, "Implicit Theories of Intelligence Predict Achievement across an Adolescent Transition: A Longitudinal Study and an Intervention," *Child Development,* forthcoming.

48. This initiative, "Improving Interethnic Relations among Youth: A School-Based Project Involving Educators, Parents, and Youth," was made possible with funding from the Carnegie Corporation of New York.

49. This course was developed and first offered in 1993 to suburban educators participating in the METCO program, a voluntary school-desegregation program in the Boston area. For more information about the development of this course, and its impact on those teachers, see Sandra M. Lawrence and Beverly Daniel Tatum, "Teachers in Transition: The Impact of Antiracist Professional Development on Classroom Practice," *Teachers College Record* 99, no. 1 (fall 1997), pp. 162–78.

50. This framework was adapted from the 1985 work of Enid Lee, *Letters to Marcia: A Teacher's Guide to Anti-Racist Education* (Toronto: Cross-Cultural Communication Centre).

51. Because participants sometimes work collaboratively in groups to develop the action plans, the total number of plans is smaller than the total number of participants.

52. Glenn E. Singleton and Curtis Linton, *Courageous Conversations about Race: A Field Guide for Achieving Equity in Schools* (Thousand Oaks, Calif.: Corwin, 2006), 245.

53. Ibid., 247.
54. Ibid., 248.
55. Ibid., 252–53.

CHAPTER THREE: "WHAT KIND OF FRIENDSHIP IS THAT?": THE SEARCH FOR AUTHENTICITY, MUTUALITY, AND SOCIAL TRANSFORMATION IN CROSS-RACIAL RELATIONSHIPS

1. Emily Bernard, ed., *Some of My Best Friends: Writings on Interracial Friendships* (New York: Amistad, 2004).
2. David Mura, "Secret Colors," in *Some of My Best Friends*, ed. Bernard 130.
3. Jean Baker Miller, "Connections, Disconnections, and Violations," Work in Progress no. 33 (Wellesley, Mass.: Stone Center Working Paper Series, 1988).
4. Ibid.
5. Emily Bernard, "Crossing the Line: An Introduction" in *Some of My Best Friends,* ed. Bernard, 6.
6. Mura, "Secret Colors," 152.
7. See Beverly Daniel Tatum, *"Why Are All the Black Kids Sitting Together in the Cafeteria?"; and Other Conversations about Race* (New York: Basic Books, 1997).
8. I owe much of my understanding of this point to the work of Janet E. Helms, ed., *Black and White Racial Identity: Theory, Research, and Practice* (Westport, Conn.: Greenwood, 1990).
9. William E. Cross Jr., *Shades of Black: Diversity in African American Identity* (Philadelphia: Temple University Press, 1991).
10. We agreed that, had our son made a similar remark about an ethnic group at someone else's house, we would want to know about it, and on that basis we decided to speak to the friend's father even though we did not know him well enough to know what his response would be. Fortunately he responded with gratitude at being told about the incident.
11. Trey Ellis, "Repellent Afro," in *Some of My Best Friends,* ed. Bernard, 83–95.
12. Ibid., 91.

13. Mura, "Secret Colors," 135–36.
14. Andrea Ayvazian and Beverly Daniel Tatum, "Women, Race and Racism: A Dialogue in Black and White," Work in Progress no. 65 (Wellesley, Mass.: Stone Center Working Paper Series, 1994).
15. Bill Ayers, "When We Were Friends: A Geography Lesson," in *Some of My Best Friends,* ed. Bernard, 96–97; 114.
16. Bernard, "Crossing the Line," 9.
17. Ayvazian and Tatum, "Women, Race, and Racism."
18. Gloria Ladson-Billings, *The Dreamkeepers: Successful Teachers of African American Children* (San Francisco: Jossey-Bass, 1994).
19. Troy Duster, "The Diversity of California at Berkeley: An Emerging Reformulation of 'Competence' in an Increasingly Multicultural World," in *Beyond a Dream Deferred: Multicultural Education and the Politics of Excellence,* ed. Becky W. Thompson and Sangeeta Tyagi (Minneapolis: University of Minnesota Press, 1993).
20. Study Circles Resource Center, *Facing Racism in a Diverse Nation: A Guide for Public Dialogue and Problem Solving* (Pomfret, Conn.: Study Circles Resource Center, 2006), www.studycircles.org.

CHAPTER FOUR: IN SEARCH OF WISDOM:
HIGHER EDUCATION FOR A CHANGING DEMOCRACY

1. T. S. Eliot, "Choruses from 'The Rock,'" in *Collected Poems, 1909–1935* (New York: Harcourt, Brace, 1936), 179.
2. For an in-depth discussion of mental health issues on college campuses, see Richard Kadison and Theresa Foy DiGeronimo, *College of the Overwhelmed: The Campus Mental Health Crisis and What to Do about It* (San Francisco: Jossey-Bass, 2004).
3. Louis Menand, "Reimagining Liberal Education," in *Education and Democracy: Re-imagining Liberal Learning in America,* ed. Robert Orrill (New York: College Entrance Exam Board, 1997).
4. Lee Knefelkamp and Carol Geary Schneider, "Education for a World Lived in Common with Others," in *Education and Democracy,* ed. Orrill, 340.
5. Charles T. Clotfelter, *After Brown: The Rise and Retreat of School*

Desegregation (Princeton, N.J.: Princeton University Press, 2004), 159.

6. Association of American Colleges and Universities, *Liberal Education Outcomes: A Preliminary Report on Student Achievement in College* (Washington, D.C., 2005).

7. Silvia Hurtado, "Reaffirming Educators' Judgment: Educational Value of Diversity," *Liberal Education* 85, no. 2 (1999), 24–31.

8. Patricia Gurin et al., "Diversity and Higher Education: Theory and Impact on Educational Outcomes," *Harvard Educational Review* 72, no. 3 (2002), 330–66.

9. Expert report of Patricia Gurin, included in University of Michigan, *The Compelling Need for Diversity in Higher Education,* reports prepared for *Gratz et al. v. Bollinger et al.* No. 97-75231 (E.D. Mich.) and *Grutter et al. v. Bollinger et al.* No. 97-75928 (E.D. Mich), www.vpcomm.umich.edu/admissions/research/.

10. Lawrence H. Summers, Remarks at NBER Conference on Diversifying the Science & Engineering Workforce, Cambridge, Mass., January 14, 2005, www.president.harvard.edu/speeches/20w05/nber.html.

11. Patricia Gurin, Brian Nagda, and G. Lopez, "The Benefits of Diversity in Education for Democratic Citizenship," *Journal of Social Issues* 60, no. 1 (2004), 17–34.

12. Linda Christensen, "Where I'm From: Inviting Students' Lives into the Classroom," in *Rethinking our Classrooms: Teaching for Equity and Justice*, vol. 2 (Milwaukee: Rethinking Schools, 2001), 6–10.

13. Beverly Daniel Tatum, "Talking about Race, Learning about Racism: The Application of Racial Identity Development Theory in the Classroom," *Harvard Educational Review* 62, no. 1 (1992), 1–24.